# Best of FST!

## Female StoryTellers Anthology
## Volume 1

### Edited by
### Melanie C. Madden & Leigh D.C. Spencer

FinnLady Press

.Published by: Janet Scott McDaniel
FinnLady Press

ISBN-10: 1548738832
ISBN-13: 978-1548738839

Printed in the United States of America
ALL RIGHTS RESERVED

FST! logo © Jennifer Mead
Front cover art © Adela Antoinette
Artwork, page 24 © Stephanie Carlson
Artwork, page 47 © Melissa Kerr
Artwork, page 58 © Sam Gilmore
Artwork, page 72 © Kylie Myers
Artwork, page 82 © Jennifer Mead
Artwork, page 90 © Jamie Keeran
Artwork, page 100 © Adela Antoinette
Artwork, page 112 © Kylie Myers
Artwork, page 128 © Amaris Diaz
Artwork, page 142 © Stephanie Carlson
Artwork, page 162 © Kylie Myers
Artwork, page 176 © Kylie Myers
Artwork, page 212 © Jennifer Mead
Artwork, page 218 © Jennifer Mead
Artwork, page 227 © Stephanie Carlson

## Dedication

This book is dedicated to our 100-plus FSTers who have graced our stage and all those yet to come.
Also, to our growing community of supporters.

4

# Acknowledgements

This book would not have been possible without the contribution of time, talent, and energy from dozens of storytellers, volunteers, and executive board members who kept FST! going throughout the years, as well as the hundreds of audience members who have shown up month after month to support our endeavor.

And, of course, we owe the biggest debt of gratitude to the visionary women who founded FST! - Female StoryTellers - and made this anthology possible! Our thanks extends to every FST!er and FST! supporter - past, present, and future.

Melanie C. Madden and Leigh D.C. Spencer, Editors

# Best of FST!

## Female StoryTellers Anthology
## Volume 1

# Table of Contents

Hi!

Welcome to The Best of FST! Female StoryTellers Anthology. We're so glad you decided to join us!

Our story begins in 2012, when a badass group of friends in Tucson came together to create a safe, magical platform where women could express themselves through the gift of storytelling. And what a gift it is! For storytellers, taking the FST! stage provides a gift of freedom,perspective, and empowerment. For our audience, every performance is a chance to receive the gifts of inspiration, compassion, and community. Not a bad way to spend an evening, right?

The FST! (pronounced "fist!") formula is simple: each month, a different theme is provided and women are invited to craft and submit a 10-15 minute story, giving life—a snapshot of their life—to that theme. At each show, five or six storytellers bring creativity, courage and provocation to their interpretations of the prompt, and the subject matter is limitless. FST! stories have explored just about every avenue you can imagine and, when you run out of road, they teach you to fly.

Storytellers discover that stepping into honest vulnerability in a public space brings empowerment. From the women who never, ever thought they could do something like this, yet bravely take the stage (sometimes more than once), to the listeners in our audience who laugh or cry or both while shouting a resounding "Me too!" FST! makes us stronger. It's contagious. It's addictive. It's beautiful. It's FST!.

Since the very first show on September 25, 2012, with rented chairs at LoveSmack Studios, where the walls shake when the train passes by, FST! has hosted more than 50 shows, featuring over 100 Female StoryTellers who have told nearly 300 brave, wacky, heart-wrenching, life-changing, hilarious stories.

These days, FST! shows are one Wednesday night a month at The Flycatcher, our home at 4th Avenue and 6th Street since 2013. As our FST!erhood (and fan base) has grown, so have FST!'s contributions to the Tucson community. FST! donates 70% of our take at the door to a different local nonprofit at each of our shows. To date, FST! has supported over 50 community organizations in Tucson. The modest amounts we have been able to raise each month add up over time: so far, we have donated over $17,000.

Not bad for our first five years.

If you're local to Tucson, we hope to see you at our show – on stage, in the ever-growing crowd, or BOTH. If you're enjoying FST! from afar, consider starting a group of female storytellers in your area. When women share their truths, it is a real, strong, and palpable magic. Make it happen!

THANK YOU for celebrating this special anniversary with us! Enjoy the Anthology – a collection of some of our favorite FST! moments (so far). Raise your voice, and your fist, as needed. Above all, welcome to the FST!erhood.

Much Love,

Melanie Madden and Leigh Spencer, Editors


P.S. One of the great things about live performance in storytelling is the immediacy of feedback—positive AND negative. Dialogue like this helps us grow as storytellers and as people! If you have reactions or feedback you'd like to share with our editors about any these stories, please drop us a line at book@fstorytellers.com.

P.P.S. Stay tuned for Best of FST! Female StoryTellers, Volume 2.

# Part 1: Identity
## *Who We Are*

There is no such thing as a "universal" women's experience. While the storytellers of FST! (we call ourselves "FST!ers") come together each month to share their stories based on a common theme, what is often remarkable is how widely our lived experiences vary.

At almost any FST! show, you can pretty much guarantee that one storyteller will be approached by a member of the audience who feels compelled to communicate just how strongly they could relate to the story that was shared onstage. Oftentimes, that sense of recognition or connection comes with a side of shock or surprise, relief and/or gratitude: *I thought I was the only one; I've never heard anyone talk about this out in the open; Thank you so much for having the courage to speak about this; It helps to know I'm not alone.*

Melanie Madden
## "The Show Must Go On" August 2015

Tonight we have a very special show. Not like, a very special episode of Blossom-special, but it's special to me. Tonight is my second FST!iversary. In August 2013, I told my first story on the FST! stage for the "Shameless" show, only it wasn't on this stage, it was at Beowulf Alley, which did not serve liquor. And I read my story. Off of paper. Which was shaking, because I was so nervous.

We've come a long way, baby.

Now Beowulf Alley is Johnny Gibson's Downtown Market, and when I marvel at how much work it must've taken to renovate a theater into a grocery store, at what an incredible transformation that is in just two years, I think—wait a minute. I've changed a lot in the last two years, too.

Two years ago, when I told my first FST! story, I was a student. Now I have my MFA and a full-time job. My job has nothing to do with creative writing, but I just took a paid vacation and—that shit is awesome. I got my normal paycheck after I didn't go to work for a week and a half. It's glorious.

Back when I told my first FST! story, I had no literary publications. I now have three. Also, my hair is longer now.

When I told my first FST! story, despite the fact that I was a student in an elite creative writing MFA program, I wasn't sure if I belonged on this stage. I was afraid I was too highfalutin'. Too academic, too verbose. And, to be fair, I was. But the FST!ers welcomed me into the FST!erhood anyways, and helped me learn how to scale back my braniac when it doesn't serve the story. And I became a better storyteller for it.

Two years ago, when I told my first FST! story, I was knock-kneed and trembling. I have told ten stories since, growing in confidence

15

each time. Now I am acting as the chair of FST!'s storytelling committee, and nothing has ever made me happier or prouder—except seeing my son's Eagle Scout ceremony. Which I told a story about, at FST!

When I told that story about my son's Eagle Scout ceremony, I wondered how long it would be before Boy Scout Leadership would lift their ban on gay leaders. That was a year and a half ago.

We've come a long way, baby.

Tonight's show is also very special to me because live performance and theater have been a huge part of my life for as long as I can remember—I distinctly remember how pumped I was to take the stage at my kindergarten graduation, with the rest of my class, when we sang some song about rainbows, with simple choreography, and I put my five-year-old all into it. I did school plays and drama club all throughout elementary, junior high and high school, so the theatrical commandment "The Show Must Go On" is as ingrained in me as the Catholicism I was raised on.

Live theater has always been a sort of second church to me, and when I left the church, drama became a way to fill that void: a place to come together as a community to listen to stories about what it means to be human.

Sadly, when I got to college and realized I wasn't the hot shit actor I thought I was in high school, I gave up on theater. I started to notice that writing was where my talent really shined, and since I wasn't the funniest, or the best, then fuck it, I wasn't even going to try. I'll just be a poet. Then when I realized I wasn't even the hot shit poet I thought I was, I gave that up, too. Fuck it, I'll just be an academic. Guess I'm just not cut out to be an artist.

And that was my 20s. Then in my mid-30s, I decided to get involved with musical theater. I sucked at it, but that didn't take away from my joy in doing it. I was almost certainly the worst singer and dancer in the ensemble of our community theater production of

Singin' in the Rain, but it was a triumph for me, all the same, because I fucking did it, when before I had convinced myself that I was incapable. I didn't take dance lessons when I was a kid and I can't read music; that anyone would ever cast me in a production of a musical seemed absurd.

It took me three auditions to be cast in a show at the Davis Musical Theater Company, but it happened. And it was hard work; it is hard work being that terrible. I sometimes cried on my bike ride home from the theater, remembering how stupid I'd looked at rehearsal. I wanted to quit, a lot. But I couldn't break the commandment, "The Show Must Go On." So I saw it through to the end, and on opening night, when we danced in our rain slickers with our umbrellas in the great big finale, we got a standing ovation, and I thought about all those teary, snot-filled late night bike commutes and thought, worth it.

That experience helped me to realize JUST how stupid the "I won't try anything unless I can be the greatest at it" ethos of my 20s was. And that's when I realized that, duh, I AM an artist, and that, duh, if I ever hope to get any good at my art, I have to be willing to spend plenty of time sucking at it first. Because that's how art works. The most successful aren't always the most talented, just the ones willing to do the work, even when it sucks.

If that last part sounds familiar, it's because I'm paraphrasing Ira Glass (and you are an NPR-listening nerd).

My run of Singin' in the Rain happened five years ago, and I think it's fitting that I told my first FST! story about that experience. Sticking it out through Singin' in the Rain helped spark a creative rebirth in me—it reminded me of how willing I was to consider myself a poet and an artist once, and of how much joy I get from being creative. It also reminded me of how much time and hard work has to go into making something you can be proud of. And that's when it finally clicked with me that I could be a writer, an artist, a real artist; all I have to do is do the work. So I joined a creative nonfiction workshop, and I started spending less time watching TV and more time reading and writing, and before long I was quitting my job and moving to Tucson to pursue an MFA.

17

And it wasn't long after that that I went to my first FST! show and knew I had to be a part of this girl gang, this radical band of truth-tellers who managed to fuse together my two passions of writing true stories, and hamming it up on stage.

Tonight is a very special show not just because it is my second anniversary show, but because this is a FST! show—five women are going to get up here and tell their truth, and they are going to do it artfully. It is hard work, but it is so rewarding.

If I seem like a late-night infomercial right now, *The power of storytelling changed my life! Call now to see what it can do for you!* that is because you're goddamn right I believe the power of storytelling changes lives. Our country is suffering from a critical lack of truth because we keep hearing the same stories over and over from cultural gatekeepers who only present the versions of stories that teach us how to keep the powerful powerful and the disenfranchised disenfranchised.

Right now it feels like political discourse in America at an absolute stalemate, and the only way we can ever hope to move forward is by learning how to listen to each other's stories, even when that means listening when a story challenges our most deeply-held beliefs, or makes us feel uncomfortable. These aren't easy things to do, listening without being defensive, listening when your beliefs are being challenged, but they get easier with practice. Just like making art. You suck at it at first, but that's not a reason to give up.

So thank you, to all of you in tonight's audience, for being here, for supporting FST!, and for practicing the art of listening; you are making the world a better place. Thank you Flycatcher, for giving us space to accommodate all these lovely people, plus lights, a mic, and a stage, not to mention your $1 vodka specials (please tip your bartenders!). Thank you ASL interpreters, for making our stories more accessible, and thank you FST!ers—past, present, and future—for bringing your truth to our stage and making every show a very special show.

**FST!** Athena Hagen-Krause
## "Next Chapter" January 2014

This story does not "begin" with my trip to see the Oracle 'cause it's one of those stories that starts way back during my gypsy feminist/theatre-fag childhood and ends who knows where… somewhere in the future.

This story doesn't begin with my trip to see the Oracle, but that is where I found my place…

You know when you're reading a book and you're tired or distracted so you keep misreading the same sentence over and over and having to go back and read it again? Or you lose your place and start where you thought you left off, but really it's the same shit you just read and you can't quite remember where you were so you go ahead and keep reading, hoping you'll stumble upon something new… eventually. That was where I was when my friend told me about her clairvoyant grandma.

(In case you're wondering, yes, "Going to See the Oracle" was sort of like that scene in The Matrix. But with fewer cookies… and I didn't break anything.)

Before we even sat down to go over my astrological chart she said to me, "Oh honey, you're all over the place."

I couldn't argue. I mean, who goes to a Fortuneteller when they have their shit together? Still, as someone who'd always worked hard at being "stable" and "grounded," it sucked to have a total stranger tell me how lost I was.

So, first off, I'd just broken up with my boyfriend of four years on what seemed to be a whim. I was still living with him in the house we'd bought together only six months before. He was kind and devoted and took care of me and the bills. Besides the house, we had a little dog, a fat cat, two cars, and a giant TV with premium cable.

This wasn't the first time I'd met a man who wanted to settle down but it was the closest I'd come to the fully accessorized American Dream.

I was more well-fed and financially secure than I'd ever been in my life, yet I felt hungry and weak and anxious all the time. I cried at night and watched "Say Yes to the Dress" marathons during the day. I took to chatting with other men behind his back. I blamed boredom and work stress and low blood sugar and his reluctance to propose.

Somewhere, I'd lost my connection to all the things that really inspired me.

Art. Friends. Work. Sex. Soul.

I'd always loved my hometown but, suddenly, I began to feel this urgency, this intense pull away from where I was... I'd never been out of the country, never really lived anywhere besides Tucson. I wanted to travel and meet new people and learn another language and do SOMETHING with my life. I didn't know what exactly, but being a housewife wasn't it. So I'd hopped back to the other side of the white picket fence and now I was sitting across from this oracle lady, desperate to find another path to.... Home.

So, yeah, it was pretty safe to say I was "all over the place," but the Oracle's next assertion was a bit harder to confirm. "Oh, but you'll be ok," she said to me and her eyes got all bright and twinkly, "You're a magical unicorn priestess."

I cringed and my mother's words interjected in my head "GAY. Oh my god. Unicorn what? This bitch is obviously crazy."

I needed something to guide me out of this limbo state so I decided to breathe and ignore the Unicorn comment and try to be open to what this lady had to say. She went over my chart and told me a lot of things I already knew about my life. It was uncanny actually, and I went back and forth between being reassured by it and totally creeped out. She spoke mostly of my present and what motivated me and what

I was searching for, these things that I'd forgotten and suppressed and dismissed.

And, of course, (being an oracle) she threw in a couple prophecies here and there for good measure:

• I would stop living for OR against my mother and start to come into my own.

• My work was a driving force in my life and it would lead me to travel the world.

• I would find a deep connection with a passionate, creative man.

• And I would be able to have the family and the sense of home that I NEEDED without the traps or trappings of tradition.

As she told me these things, I was amazed at how precisely she'd articulated my "wildest" and most "unrealistic" dreams, the ones I'd been trying so hard to let go of in order to become a "grown up."

So now I had this outline of what my life could look like. But where to actually begin? Or had I begun already? And then again, should I really even trust some weirdo hippy lady who repeatedly insisted that I was a "Unicorn Priestess"?

It was all rather confusing.

For some reason, the Unicorn thing really stuck with me…

I started noticing Unicorns everywhere, farting glitter and vomiting rainbows. They were so cute and kitschy. Something that little girls and little old ladies loved in a sincere way and hipsters loved in an ironic way and most people regarded as a total joke. And THAT was supposed to be my fuckin' power animal? Ugh.

But then I remembered The Last Unicorn. As a kid, my mom used to read the book to me and I'd watched the movie at least million times. THIS was a version of the creature that I could relate to.

21

If you're not familiar with the story, I don't want to spoil anything for you… But, I'm going to anyway. It's about a unicorn who leaves the safety of her forest to venture out into the unknown in search of others of her kind. But, just as she's coming close to finding the other unicorns, she's transformed into a human girl.

She meets a prince who falls madly in love with her and she starts to forget her true nature and her quest. Luckily, her two traveling companions, (a bungling magician and a cynical older woman) remind her of her purpose. Then she has to face her fears and confront "The Red Bull" and rescue all the other unicorns in the world from a fate worse than death!

It's pretty epic!

I remember watching the movie for the first time in years, sitting on the couch in front of that big-screen TV and thinking: "Holy crap! This soundtrack is ridiculous." And also—"This is totally the story of my life." As I read the novel, I thought "Well. Shit. I guess I really am a Unicorn." And it dawned on me then that the reason that I'd been feeling so lost for so long was that I'd been trying to find my place in a completely different story than the one I was actually living. I could make my way to the castle with the adoring prince just fine, but somehow I'd always lose my place, put down my book and pick up some Disney Princess bullshit. I kept thinking I'd found the wrong Prince, but really, it was just the wrong book.

So, along with what the Oracle had told me, The Last Unicorn became like a map back to my true path. The prophecies were my landmarks, my destination and the book gave me detailed instructions on how to get there.

Of course, if you've ever tried to use a map, you know that having a map and making the journey are very different things. Real life doesn't always match up with the diagram. The route I'm taking isn't always easy; it can be grueling and painful and lonely at times, but having that vision, that storyline to follow has kept me going even when things looked hopeless or pointless or totally insane. I've come to accept the role of "Unicorn Priestess" with pride. As I search for the others, I find myself and I am often forced to confront the things that I am most afraid of. I know I must be on the right track because, one by one, the things the oracle spoke of have started to come true and the dreams I once held secret have started to materialize; many times as if by magic, other times as if by mistake, but most of the time as if they were simply the next chapter in the story.

This summer, while traveling for work, I made a deep connection with a passionate, creative man. He speaks no English, so I've had to learn a new language. And I've got my passport and my plane ticket because, in two weeks, I'll be taking my very first trip out of the US.

I still have moments of forgetting and moments of living for and against my mother. There are times when I lose my place on the page and have to review, times when I lose my place on the map and have to take a detour. But I'm learning to trust the people I meet and to trust that the story knows where it's going even when I feel lost. And if coming this far has taught me anything at all, it's that there are always lessons hiding in the out-of-the-way and in-between places. So after years spent finding my place and making my way through this crucial chapter, I think I'm finally ready to turn the page.

Female StoryTellers Presents:

FST!

Wednesday,
June 18th
7:00 pm
(doors @ 6:30)

$7 Suggested
Donation (cash only)
Proceeds Benefit:
BICAS

The Flycatcher
340 E 6th St
*21+ Venue
ASL Interpreters
Provided

Best Summer Ever

www.fstorytellers.com

# FST! Thea
## "Best Summer Ever" June 2014

Back in the summer of 2006, I decided to become an Indian. I was in school, studying art, and I found myself with the whole summer off because I needed to move out of the artist's retreat near Napa, California, before the new round of summer artists arrived. One day, a thought just popped into my head—go learn to weave baskets. Sure, there are jokes about getting college credit for underwater basket weaving. But I am a member of the Jicarilla Apache Nation and Jicarilla means "little basket." We are a tribe of basket weavers.

The thing is, I'm only half Jicarilla and I grew up in Los Angeles, where most of my closest friends were white. I knew nothing about being an Indian. As a child, my mom took me to the odd powwow now and again, and every summer we'd head to New Mexico so my mom could visit her family. Her family. My sister and I had fun on the rez, running around in the dirt and playing with the many puppies that popped up at my grandparent's house every summer. When I look at pictures of those times, I see my sister and me as we stand beneath a clothesline in clean, pressed city clothes, standing out like sore thumbs.

I didn't know the first thing about weaving baskets, but, lucky for me, my mom's cousin had been in charge of the tribal Arts and Crafts Museum for over forty years. I called Gladys and explained who I was. "I know who you are!" said Gladys quite loudly. Then, Gladys told me about the tribal summer student employment program—I was going to learn to weave baskets and get paid!

In my excitement, I called my friend Alicia who lives on the reservation with her monghanii husband and her two beautiful children. While Alicia, who herself has woven a number of baskets, was very supportive of my learning to weave, she did feel compelled to warn me, "You're not tough enough for the rez!" I explained that I grew up in Los Angeles—I'm not exactly naive or idealistic. Alicia just laughed.

25

My mother spent the first eighteen years of her life on the reservation. She now lives in Los Angeles as she has for over fifty years. Although she hasn't always been, my mother had become an optimistic and loving parent. She felt compelled to warn me: "When those ladies say mean things to you, don't say anything back. Just ignore them and weave your basket. Don't say anything back to them when they say mean things." When they say mean things?

Those warnings did not give me second thoughts; I tend to be bull-headed and determined. I mentioned my summer plans to the owner of the Napa artist retreat when she came in to prepare the retreat center for the new crop of artists. Sophia was originally from England and owned artist retreats in both California and New Zealand. "If I can offer you any advice," said Sophia as she heartily scrubbed the stovetop, "it's to remember that when you go to another country, and for you an Indian reservation is another country, remember that they know everything about life there and how things work, and that you know nothing."

As I drove onto the reservation about two weeks later, I was wearing cut-off shorts and my light pink Gap t-shirt. I soon found out that no one wears short-shorts on the rez. Despite the heat, people wear jeans, and younger people, both girls and boys, favor those long, satiny basketball shorts, like the type the L.A. Lakers wear. On the reservation, an unfamiliar face is always news—a fresh puzzle to figure out, and fodder for gossip. I stood out a little bit, I think.

Those first few days, I visited the many tribal trailer/offices and the rec center that I vaguely remember from the annual summer visits of my childhood. I dropped into the Arts & Crafts Museum to say hello to my mom's cousin Gladys.

I was staying with my cousin's dad, Ralph. I walked into his trailer after spending the day exploring the little town. Ralph was a white man, a monghaani who married an Apache woman and adopted my cousin Laura. I told Ralph about exploring the small town, about the horses at the river, and that Gladys wanted me to start on Monday at 8 a.m.

"Eight in the morning?" Ralph asked, "I guarantee you one thing, NO ONE who works for the tribe is gonna get there at EIGHT in the morning!"

I arrived at 8 a.m. sharp Monday morning and Gladys told me to wait until the rest of the employees arrived. Waiting meant standing around. Literally, I stood. I examined the beadwork and baskets in the display case. I peeked into the room where the bead workers and basket weavers worked. A sole woman sat sewing beads to a round piece of buckskin. I think she noticed me, but she did not look up.

I watched the curious faces of about five other women as they trickled in, noticing me, but quickly looking away. After about forty-five minutes, Gladys announced that we were all going out to breakfast. Breakfast at 9 a.m. after we'd clocked in. We went to one of the only restaurants in town, a diner attached to the local Best Western hotel. We arrived back at the Arts & Crafts Museum about an hour before lunch. Gladys told me that after lunch, I would go out to cut willow and sumac with Lyn, a youngish woman with waist-length hair who smiled when she met me.

So there is an art form to knowing where the best, straightest, and right-sized willows are. After lunch, Lyn informed me that most weavers had their own secret willow-harvesting locations. Lyn drove the new, white, department Chevy Suburban to a spot about a mile from town. Lyn slowed down then stopped the vehicle every now and again. Sometimes, Lyn told me to go out to see if the willows there grew straight and tall. Sometimes, we stopped to harvest some willow with our sharp paring knives, other times Lyn drove slowly, looking, looking for willow perfection. After a couple of hours of stopping, harvesting and loading into the back of the tribal Suburban, we headed back to the museum.

I was sitting shotgun as we drove back toward town along the river when I noticed a large fish on the side of the road. It looked over a foot long and seemed as though it had jumped out of the small stream for unknown reasons and ended up lying, resting on the side of the road. I thought it was funny and told Lyn. She stopped the truck.

"What did it look like?" asked Lyn with a serious expression.

"It was silver and about this big," I said, holding my palms a littleover a foot apart.

"What kind was it?" Lyn asked.

"I don't know what kind. It was like a big fish," I said.

Lyn put the Suburban in reverse and I stuck my head out the window to make sure Lyn didn't back up over the fish. She stopped the vehicle and we both got out. We walked around to the passenger side and stood staring down at the fish, which looked silvery and fresh.

"What do you think?" I asked, looking at Lyn, who stood silently looking at the fish.

"You can't eat those," said Lyn as she headed back into the truck.

Basket weaving. Basket weaving is hard work. The willow and sumac has to be split and soaked and even just starting a basket from the very bottom center was so hard that it took me half a day to make what amounted to a basket the size of a half-dollar coin. After spending each day weaving, I went back to Ralph's trailer with my hands aching. My thumbs were so sore from weaving that I couldn't even flip the light switch off. Or on. And don't even get me talking about trying to unbutton my jeans without using my painful thumbs.

But I loved it. I just loved it.

Sometimes, the other basket weavers and I listened to drum music first thing in the morning, courtesy of the local public radio station, or we sat for hours weaving in silence. And the ladies gradually warmed up to me. And none of those wonderful, talented, and wise artisans ever said anything mean to me.

The thing is, I can't say that I learned to be an Indian, whatever that means. For me, I think that being a Jicarilla Apache is reserved for people who grew up on the reservation and lived there all their lives. Then, of course, there are urban Indians, which could be a category that I would fit into; if I were an Indian.

I still don't feel like an Indian, but I do know a little bit more about life, ritual, and culture on the reservation. For me, this was the best summer job ever because I learned to sit and weave my basket in silence, to be patient and run on Indian time. I learned to eat mutton stew and, somewhere along the way, I connected with these wonderful, talented bead workers and basket weavers. They weren't the family I was looking for, but they are still family to me. Years later, I still don't feel like an Indian or an artist, but back then in the summer of 2006, I knew exactly who I was.

**FST!** Alexx Ramirez

## "Parents Just Don't Understand" June 2016

I wasn't a terribly social child. At least, not the way of so many children I knew who were that adorable, cutesy, polite, everyone-loves-them kind of social. I pretty much hated kids my own age. I preferred to spend my time in the company of senior citizens.

At first, my maternal unit thought it was cute that my best friends were the sweet old couple who lived next door to us. But it worried her, too. Not only was I not-hanging out with kids my own age, but where kids my own age were at soccer games, I was with senior citizens at funerals or cribbage games. I was a quiet little child with a fascination for war: playing Pearl Harbor with stuffed animals and checking with my war veteran friends to make sure the re-enactments were accurate.

My mom worried the worries and hoped the hopes of a first-time mom, who was both a single mother by day and a prison guard by night.

So, at the same time she had a hope chest in her heart full of my potential to be the president of the United States when I grew up, she also had a despair chest full of many fears and worries. Her many worries included the tiny prickling worry that one day I would grow up to be a psychopath.

Maybe that's a fear all parents have. Your parents had that fear, right? Okay, maybe not.

At some point, my mom decided it would be good and healthy for her daughter to play with kids her own age, stop attending so many funerals, and find non-violent activities to occupy her mind.

And so it was that my mother sent me off to summer camp. I imagine when she saw the camp brochure, she saw this wholesome leftover from the heyday of summer camps in the late 1950's. She

30

saw a beautiful island in the middle of a lake that must have reminded her of a happier time and the 1961 Disney classic, The Parent Trap. She must have thought it was the perfect place to send her socially-challenged tween daughter. It was the perfect place, but for reasons she did not understand then and probably does not understand now.

Happily for me, camp had its own version of a back room for VIP poker players. The adorable, blissfully innocent children had their parent-pleasing activities out front for all to see. But after my counselors realized I was not happy with my pre-planned schedule and that I had a talent for certain other activities like pyromania, I left ceramics and dance and took up archery, metalcraft, and campcraft. Campcraft was just a cutesy code-name name for wilderness survival. I got to sleep outside and learn how to build fires.

Really, really big fires.

One of our counselors told us that underestimation was one of our best weapons. "People never expect the Spanish inquisition," she said, and "They won't expect a group of socially awkward 12-year-olds to know how to cut, shoot, dig, bury, burn, and walk away."

Maybe those weren't her exact words, but looking around, I was sure that was the message all of us got.

At dinner one night, the director bade the staff and campers to wish my cabin well on our overnight adventures. They were camping at the beach. I was off to camp in the wild. So we sang our traditional camp songs of encouragement. The last one of the night was about a Jewish wife burning down a candy store to fraudulently collect insurance proceeds.

I started out on my adventure to the Outback, which was an area outside the main boundaries of camp marked by several coyote skulls and a mishmash of rodent bones where the campcrafters who came before had been sent with a bag of kindling, a knife, and a Charleston chew bar. Some of their bones would be in the woods, too, and their spirits would watch over us—or so we were told.

My mission was to build a shelter, make a fire from wet wood, and forage for food. The main goal, though, was to survive, by any means necessary, for a night and part of a day, in the woods, alone.

At first, I could hear my cabin mates, who were camped just about a half-mile away at the beach. They sang lullabies until it was lights out time for them, and fire building time for me.

I had carefully, painstakingly set up a tall triangular fire lay (called a teepee structure) with poisonous hemlock, rotted pine branches, scraps of wet birch bark, and a can of gasoline I found by the boat dock.

It was my own personal heaven, something like where Max from Where the Wild Things Are joins up with the cast from Lord of the Flies in a musical ensemble.

Except there wasn't anybody else. It was just me. And I didn't build a shelter because I didn't need to sleep. I had a 12 foot tall wall of fire and the charred bits of my Charleston Chew bar to entertain me.

I felt, for the first time, like I had found my place. I found somewhere I belonged and somewhere I fit in. And sure, that place was alone, by myself, with a fire, in the woods. But hey, there was a place. And, in my defense, it had people on the edges, like half a mile away. It was a good distance away. It still is.

After the sun came up, I trekked back to the edge of the beach where my cabinmates greeted me with chocolate chip and banana pancakes because they really were some of the best teacup-sized humans on the planet. It was a bittersweet morning because we had only a few hours before the ferry would take us back to civilization. We all said our goodbyes and our counselors armed us with "final report cards." Mine extolled my social progress, tidy bunk, and close friends. It mentioned how the outdoors seemed to agree with me and, of course, enclosed my award for badminton. My mom was thrilled with how much I loved camp. She was ecstatic that I was learning to be a socially responsible, socially social person with socialness. And friends! My own age!

You might think the story ends there, because, you know, parents just don't understand. But looking back on some of my mom's memorable mom moments says a lot about what she did and didn't understand.

When I was 18 and got my first tattoo, a dolphin jumping out of wave (clearly the sign of a deranged mind), my mother was furious and pulled a lecture straight out of her prison guard despair chest. She ranted, "Do you understand that now you have a permanently identifying characteristic? Do you understand what that means?" She told me that after I escaped from jail and was on the lam, America's Most Wanted would feature my tattoos on a segment about my escape. "The whole world," she said, "is going to be able to find you. And you're going to go right back to jail. Is that you want?" That tells you something, a lot of somethings, about my mom.

Another memorable moment was when I passed the Bar Exam. "You're an attorney now!" she said. "You've studied criminal law!" she said. "You know all the tricks!" she said. "And you know some really good defense attorneys now, don't you? Like some of the best, right? And some judges?"

There was a long pause and she said, "Not like you'd get caught."

So at least she understood that much.

An earlier, happy mom moment was me getting that first "report card" from summer camp on how well-adjusted I learned to seem to be. "It seems like you were really learning to fit in!" she told me. And when I think about it now, she had the voice that the father of Dexter, the serial killer who kills serial killers, had when praising his son for blending in.

See, she just didn't understand. She didn't understand that I wasn't (at the time) some criminal mastermind. I was just an introverted, slightly morbid kid who understood at far too early an age that people

33

suck. Seriously, sometimes they're just awful and it's okay to not like awful people. At that point in my life, I didn't have coffee or bourbon to help me like people more. I only had summertime chocolate chip banana pancakes that psychotically chipper children of the corn made for me, and campfires, and the woods, and time to be by myself.

I tried explaining myself to my mom so many times and it never worked. She just didn't understand. But, she understood something incredibly important: She understood that she didn't understand me or what she thought of as my criminal predispositions. But she knew I loved summer camp and that it made me happy and she knew that she loved me and wanted me to have a place where I fit in. And so she sent me back to that summer camp for psychopaths every summer, even though that was a huge expense for a single mom on a civil servant's salary. She also started a "bail fund" jar when I came back from that first summer away, you know, just in case she really understood me and I didn't understand myself. To this day, I'm pretty sure my mom doesn't understand me. But I'm also pretty sure that it doesn't matter.

Bethany Evans
## "Never Say Never" December 2013

I woke up to a blaring alarm clock. The militant red numbers announced that it was noon. Why the hell did I have to be awake at noon? I staggered to turn off the alarm, and remembered why.

I had a work meeting in a couple hours, to collaborate on a new cocktail menu. Cocktails were the last thing I wanted to think about.

A bottle of Pinnacle vodka sat on my dresser. It was ¾ empty. It was Whipped Cream flavor.

The aftertaste in my mouth was not Whipped Cream flavor. It was Fuck-My-Life flavor. My head was pounding. Did I really drink that much Whipped Cream vodka? Who drinks Whipped Cream vodka? I could at least have had the decency to be a drunk with a discerning palate. Just thinking about the Whipped Cream vodka shots with Diet Coke-backs made my stomach turn. I ran to the bathroom to retch.

I didn't remember passing out the night before. Last night's bra was still on, and so was last night's makeup, mascara running down my face in small, sad rivers. I looked like a half-assed Juggalo.

I did the only thing I knew would make the pounding stop. I finished the bottle.

At noon. In less than twelve hours, I drank a fifth of vodka.

Surprise: instead of making me feel better, the renewed buzz made me feel worse. I hated myself. I was such a screw-up. My cat stared at me with judgmental eyes. Making sure all my curtains were closed and all daylight expelled, I decided to go back to sleep. I set my alarm for a half hour before the meeting, and hoped that by then the booze would wear off.

Surprise: I slept through the alarm.

35

Groggy and disoriented, I woke up a half hour after the meeting started. I raced to work.

Honestly, I probably wasn't okay to drive, but I wasn't making good judgment calls. The meeting was nearly over by the time I got there. After its conclusion, I pulled my co-manager aside.

"Sorry I'm late. I woke up still-drunk and did a few more shots and fell asleep, then slept through my alarm."

"Oh, B."

That was my life in my early 20s: going all Amy Winehouse on everyone, going out every single night, and bringing random people home to have random sex. Sometimes, I didn't even remember doing it. Condom wrappers serving as stand-ins for memory. There was one night when I woke up in a parking lot after blacking out. I was so reckless and self-destructive, hurling    spears at my body and spirit, seeing which ones would stick.

I had abandoned writing. I was convinced that love was out of the question. I had dated one Morrissey fan too many. During the day, I never went outside, never opened the curtains. I dreaded the outside world because people would be "onto me." I was in Hell.

There is a silver lining to being in Hell: you have nowhere to look but up.

Absurdly, my upward climb began with a bartending competition: the Guinness Perfect Pint Pour-Off. I was asked to represent my bar in the competition, where 20 bartenders from around Tucson competed in pouring the perfect pint of Guinness. I didn't want to do it. It seemed pretentious—was a 10-point rubric really necessary for pouring a beer? But mostly, I didn't want to compete because it was being hosted at an ex's bar. I figured I'd lose and embarrass myself.

During this time, I'd started dating a funny, nice guy who made breakfast and opened my curtains in the morning. He encouraged me to compete. Why not? Free beer. YOLO.

I watched YouTube videos on how to pour the perfect pint. Yes, those exist. I practiced on every customer who would let me. I even got a manicure, my nails resembling ten tiny Guinness pints.

On the big night, I went with my bosses and my coworker to the bar where it was being held. The Guinness people had set up two taps side-by-side on a stage. A news crew was setting up their cameras. There were a TON of people there, mostly bartenders and sales reps, many faces I knew. Including one face that I knew very well.

"You pouring tonight?" He asked me.

"Yep."

"Well, good luck, kiddo..."

Ugh. I had to win.

Round one. FIGHT! I approached the platform and introduced myself to my competitor. Hands trembling, I poured my first pint.

"These are the two best Guinness pints I've seen so far," one of the judges declared. "Do a tie-breaker pour now, please."

And then I won the tie-breaker round.

The night went on, and I kept beating my competitors and advancing. The crowd cheered me on.

It started to dawn on me that I might actually win-win. And then I did. Draped in the winner's jersey, clutching my trophy and blowing kisses like a big old Christmas ham, I accepted my title as Tucson's best pourer. Flushed, I told the news cameras, "The perfect pint is defined by a proud head, because Guinness drinkers are definitely proud."

Proud.

For the first time in ages, I remembered what it felt like to be proud, proud as the ¾" dome of head that topped a Guinness pint. Yes, I felt pride for something as trivial as a bartending contest, but still... I had applied effort and won something. It had been so long since I'd felt proud of anything. It was intoxicating. I never thought I'd win. Never say never.

Two months later, my friend Lauren was pestering me for the umpteenth time about FST! Female StoryTellers. I knew she and some friends had started a storytelling group, and I had, month after month, lurked their events on Facebook, but never actually gone. I was a bit mystified by "storytelling". . . like, what does that even mean?

Why would anyone want to hear my stories? My partner encouraged me to go to Table Talk, which, at the time, was where the themes for future FST! shows were decided. I decided I could handle brainstorming storytelling themes with Lauren and her friends. Why not? It would be a no-pressure way to dip my toes into the pond.

The ladies at Table Talk were friendly and inviting. They laughed at my lame jokes and encouraged me to write something for the next show, "The Road Less Travelled." Bolstered by the presence of these women, I sat down at my computer, and I wrote.

I wasn't sure if I would perform, but I went to rehearsal.

When it came time for me to read my story at rehearsal, I did that annoying thing where you apologize: "Sorry, this my first time, sorry if it sucks, sorry, I don't think I'm even going to perform, sorry, I don't have my story memorized." Then I read my story.

The feedback I received was incredible. I went into workshop feeling like I didn't belong, and left feeling like I had a story worth telling. I went home and started practicing reading out loud.

Once again, my cat stared at me with those damn judgmental eyes.

Performance night, I wore a new dress and heels and walked from my downtown house to LoveSmack Studio, my final draft folded in my sweaty hands. I brought my notes on stage with me, nervous that an actual audience would boo me off stage (because audiences totally still boo people off stage). But I went on with my story. Let me tell you, it was way scarier than pouring a freaking Guinness.

Afterward: support. People saying they could relate. My friends, who knew me but didn't know I had that in me. That was my 2nd dose of the highly addictive drug, pride. But it was more than pride. It was a sense of self-worth and creative expression.

There was catharsis in storytelling, for me and the audience. Both the teller and the listener of the story become changed. We meet halfway.

Over the months, my passion for FST! grew. I told more stories. I became involved backstage, and got to know the women in the "FST!erhood" on a closer level. The good vibes inspired me. I didn't have to draw the curtains on my life; I could pull them back and expose the cobwebs, and so what? Brooms are a thing.

At this point, I was definitely no longer feeling like a screw-up and drinking Whipped Cream vodka. I stepped up my game. I drank Jameson. No, but really, I was in love and my creativity was flourishing.

And then I took my first yoga class. Yoga helped me connect the pieces. In a very real way, I began to understand that life is practice.

I want to share something my friend Karyn said to me, when I was telling her about this story:

"Happiness isn't a permanent status, it isn't something you reach and, phew, you're done."

Happiness is something you must vigilantly protect. There is no happy ending; there is happy now. And to paraphrase my other friend, Britney Spears, if you want happy… you better work, bitch.

One year ago, I considered peeling myself off the bed to drink vodka a valid form of exercise. I never thought I'd be here, sharing my story of crawling from rock-bottom to a higher ground.

I'm definitely not at paradise yet. I still get white-girl wasted sometimes, I still neglect things like laundry, and I still haven't gotten a "real job." There's higher ground yet. Maybe the joke is, you never actually get to paradise. But I'm happy.

If you listen to the stories tonight and feel inspired to tell your own story, I hope that you do. You might think you have never been "good at public speaking" or never had anything interesting happen to you or that your story won't be good enough or you can never do it.

You can. Never say never. Try. Because it all begins with saying "Yes." Or, at the very least, "Why not?"

Becca Perry Tardiff
## "It's a Rite of Passage" December 2012

So I'm Jewish. I'm sure there are a handful of you out there that have never met a Jew before, so now you can say you've at least seen one. Growing up in Arizona I've been a lot of people's "First Jew," and it's always been an honor. I suppose in some way, I have been a rite of passage for those people who can now say they have met a Jew... and she didn't have a giant nose! (Although her eyebrows are pretty thick).

Someone told me that a rite of passage is "going from one status to another" which immediately made me think of my recent breakup. It was not a proud Facebook status update moment for me. "Becca Perry Mandel has gone from In a Relationship to Single"... ouch. I thought about sharing what I went through, but then I realized, even though I felt convinced that no one in the world could possibly know my heartache, the truth is everyone did. So I decided to share something that most of you probably haven't experienced—the rite of passage that comes with growing up as a little Jewish girl in Arizona, where the Jewish population is a whopping 1.7%. I guess it could be worse. At least it's over 1%, unlike Alabama, Arkansas, Kentucky, Louisiana... well, most of the South, basically.

I want to share some stories with you, to take you through my rite of passage that took me from being a little Jewish girl who struggled with feeling different, who felt scared at times to be Jewish, who became a total Christmas-hating Grinch, and finally to becoming a woman who embraces who she is and can actually enjoy Christmas.

Naturally, it all started with Santa. I mean how do you explain to a kid why Santa, the most exciting character around, doesn't come to their house to eat cookies and deliver presents? There's really no easy way to break it, so instead my parents made desperate attempts to get me excited about some Hanukkah Harry guy (a weak Santa replacement if you ask me) that was going to deliver my eight presents under my Hanukkah bush. Yeah, try getting pumped about decorating a bush.

Anyways, Hanukkah Harry didn't last long and I was quickly back to needing a reason to not feel so shitty that Santa didn't know where I lived. Props to my brother who had it under control. He helped me cope by teaching me the truth: Jewish parents love their children more because they buy their own presents instead of contracting out some big dude with a white beard to do it. Now, that felt good to me. I could handle that. My parents just loved me more. Screw Santa!

Unfortunately, although that was an excellent coping mechanism for me, it didn't go over well with the Christian kids I preached it to. And so it began that being Jewish meant I was different, and this difference would be highlighted, to the extreme, every year from the day after Thanksgiving to Christmas Day.

I remember the first time my mom told me to lie about Christmas. Now, this blew me away because I grew up with a core set of values, including honesty, and I felt strongly about being truthful. I remember when this honesty thing became a problem for me during a holiday season visit to the dentist. He was all up in my mouth and, with a big smile, asked me what my family was doing for Christmas. My immediate reaction was honest—I told him that I'm Jewish and my family doesn't celebrate Christmas. You would think I cursed or something by his reaction. Then I felt all awkward that I made him all awkward. And then the level of awkward just got out of control, and spiraling awkward is never a good thing. I left thinking "Hmmm... I don't want to tell anyone I'm Jewish and that I don't celebrate Christmas again".

When I expressed this to my mom, she, with all her years of wisdom and experience answering the "What are you doing for Christmas?" question, knew exactly what to say. She said, "Lie. Sometimes white lies are good." And then she helped me construct answers to a variety of Christmas-related questions so that I would be better prepared for my next encounter. This whole thing just reinforced how different I was and how my being Jewish sometimes made other people uncomfortable, which in turn made me pretty uncomfortable. I didn't like how that felt and I certainly didn't like the idea of lying to just make it easier. But I did it, because, frankly, it was easier.

In addition to feeling different because I didn't celebrate the same holidays, I soon learned that many of those stereotypes about Jews were kind of true. Like I mentioned before, I'm grateful I didn't get the big nose. But I certainly have that whole dark feature, hairy thing going on. And it was a lot more noticeable and unattractive when I was younger—pre shaving, waxing and tweezing. I didn't know how hairy my legs and arms were until my older brothers made sure I knew. I mean, that's what older brothers are for, right? I know it was poking fun out of love to relentlessly tell me that my legs were as thick as forests, but, as I looked around and saw all these blondes with fine and light hair, my insecurities became a bit overwhelming. Long story short, I definitely was the first girl in my class to shave my legs. On the up side, I no longer had hairy legs, but my brother still had a giant nose and bushy eyebrows, so the sibling tables turned with poking fun.

All of these things were rough growing up, but I soon began to learn more about my culture. I grew excited about being Jewish as I went through Hebrew school and towards a real, concrete rite of passage—being Bat Mitzvahed and becoming a woman in the eyes of the Jewish community. This was incredibly meaningful for me, as an introduction to feeling spiritual and connected to my faith. Unfortunately, this was paired with the first time I experienced real anti-Semitism. For the first time, I felt scared to be Jewish.

I was in 4th grade and my Hebrew school was tagged with swastikas. I was young, but I knew what that meant and what kind of hate someone harbored to do such a thing. Sadly, this was not the last time I felt that fear. As I grew older, I became more aware of the fact that anti-Semitism is real; it's not just this foreign thing that happened in the Holocaust. I don't know if there are police officers outside of church, but they are always outside my temple for the high holy days. And they should be. After all, there were times that Rosh Hashana or Yom Kippur services attracted bomb threats. Now that's scary shit. Someone is really going to evoke that kind of fear, just because I'm Jewish?

Just like 10 years ago, in the Tucson Foothills, a van of Neo-Nazis chased my brother down, threatening his life, just because he had a bumper sticker on the back of his car that had Hebrew letters on it. Just like the shooting at my college, driven by some Jew-hating man who journaled about wanting to kill us all before he killed one of the students because she was Jewish. I remember being overcome by this intense feeling that this shooter, still at large, would somehow find me and know that I was Jewish—just by my dark features and last name. That same fear is the reason I never got the tattoo I always wanted: Hebrew letters that said "La'chayim", which means "to life."

It's not like I live in fear on a daily basis or anything, but you never know what someone's reaction might be to seeing Hebrew. I remember being at a bar once in Flagstaff and this guy (clearly some kind of neo-Nazi) started praising Hitler and hating on Jews. My Catholic boyfriend was ready to confront him. All I wanted to do was curl up in a corner and hide. I can't explain that feeling, thinking, "This guy is fucking crazy. I don't even want to know what he is capable of."

Oy vey, this is getting intense.

How about buying my first adult menorah? This is a good story that helped to contribute to why I was a Christmas-hating Grinch. I really was. Like, if I could have stolen all the presents and made Christmas not happen, I would have done it. I had the same menorah since I was a little kid, but, once I moved out, I thought I should buy my own menorah. So, of course, I went to Target. Because they have everything. Instead of searching around for the Holiday aisles, I just asked an employee where I could fine the Hanukkah section. No joke—she looked at me and said, "Anukah??" She had no idea what I was talking about. How have you never heard of Hanukkah?

So my friend and I found our way to the Holiday section on our own. First of all, there were like fifteen Christmas aisles, so I'm not sure what this whole war on Christmas thing is. Hanukkah didn't even get one aisle. It got one of those end caps. There was one menorah and no candles left, but I made do. Now I know why people keep their menorahs once they get a good one!

I do have to say that, since then, the Hanukkah selection has drastically improved. I was really impressed with both Target and Bed Bath and Beyond this year and I look forward to seeing what new things they have next year!

Last year's Christmas was really a transformative moment for me. Like I mentioned, I was dating a Catholic and his family welcomed me to celebrate Christmas with them. It was the first real Christmas that I got to be a part of. Imagine, my whole life, I was on the outside, eating Chinese food and seeing a movie on Christmas. That year, I got to actually get presents from Santa! I didn't want to show how excited I really was, because that would make me vulnerable to the fact that my Grinchness was driven by jealousy. But I was SUPER excited! Like, little kid excited. The same kind of excitement my oldest brother had when he got to celebrate his first Christmas with his now wife. He woke up at 5am and ran down the stairs to be the first one awake for presents! He was 28.

My reaction was similar. By the end of present opening, I was wearing every possible thing I could and had a smile on my face from ear-to-ear. That child inside me that felt so rejected by Santa was finally being embraced and it felt so good.

Reflecting on the fact that I not only didn't hate Christmas, but I actually liked it was the ultimate status change for me as far as my faith. That bitterness and suppressed Grinch-like jealousy, which lingered since I was that kid on the outside, began to fade away and the Holiday season became a time of love and joy instead.

But I think there is more to this than just my rite of passage around a holiday. I tried to think about where my change of status is regarding the fear of anti-Semitism. The truth is, that fear still exists and probably always will, to a certain extent. It is the way I now view that kind of hate that has changed.

Tikkun Olam is a Hebrew phrase that means "repairing the world." It is a core belief of Judaism that resonates deeply with me. As personal as Anti-Semitism is to me, it isn't the only –ism out there; it isn't the only expression of hate, and I'm certainly not the only one that has felt this kind of fear. Instead of curling up in a corner and letting that kind of hate spread, I have embraced who I am and, with age and experience, transformed it into a place of strength, where I am prepared to help repair the world as part of a shared responsibility—hairy arms and all.

## FST! Amber Frame
### "Fish Out of Water" April 2016

I have this spiritual problem. It's not the kind that involves struggling to find the meaning in things, or figuring out the nature of reality, or what lies beyond the physical form. Nor is it about searching for a spiritual practice. I have practices. I do yoga, I do Tai chi. I meditate. I collect crystals. I drink kombucha. I talk to my plants.

So my issue maybe isn't with spirituality... it's with spiritual people. By which I mean people who say they receive "downloads." People who talk about their chakras in casual conversation. People who want to explain the nature of transcendence to me. (Which is usually men, by the way—the ones who want to not really discuss things but *explain* things. But that's a subject for another story...)

I feel like I should have a lot in common with these people, yet I always end up feeling awkward or uneasy. Like when someone you don't know very well starts telling you about something extremely personal, like a tragic event in their life, or a weird sexual fantasy. When someone starts talking to me about karma and dharma and planetary aspects, my head just spins until I'm searching for something meaningful to add, staring into their sparkly eyes until finally they pause, and I say something lame like, "yeah, totally" or, "that's heavy, man."

This is weird to me because I grew up with spirituality. My parents studied religion and philosophy. As a kid, I read books like *Be Here Now* and did yoga with my mom in the living room. When I went to visit my aunt and uncle, I didn't stay in the guest room; I stayed in the meditation room, on a little futon on the floor that was covered in cat hair and smelled like Nag Champa.

When I was little, my favorite stores were ones with names like "The Crystal Waterfall." When I was around 8 years old, I was in one of these stores, and I was told those magical childhood words: I could

48

pick out any one thing that I wanted in the store. I already knew what I wanted—a book I had had my eye on earlier, called The Missing Magical Energy. It told the story of a beautiful but sad planet earth, pained by pollution, separation, and greed—all the horrible things that make a planet weep in grey streaks of dramatic watercolor in a children's book. In the story, beings from across the galaxy representing things like courage, hope, and understanding were summoned to help planet earth, to find out what had gone wrong. What was the missing magical energy?

I'm sorry to spoil the story for anyone who has not yet read this new age children's classic, but the missing energy turned out to be love. Here, love was illustrated as rainbows—great ribbons of rainbows flowing out of windows, out of cars, out of the minds of people meditating, out of children playing, kites flying, mothers hanging laundry, people playing guitars... it was amazing. The best part was at the end, when all the beings were united and traveled back to their home planet where they met The Magical Rainbow Man—a new being who they had created through the power of their love!

At the very back of the book, there's a page where you can color in your own planet Earth, enveloped in rainbows, and send it to someone in your life who might need some love. And there's also a message from The Magical Rainbow Man. It reads, "If you'd like to be one of my special Rainbow Helpers, and know all about my new adventures, I'll keep you informed with my Secret Magical Scroll. I'll be waiting to hear from you! Love, The Magical Rainbow Man. *Send $2 plus .50c postage for your magical scroll which includes a Magical Rainbow Sticker to: The Magical Rainbow Man, Box 717, Ojai CA 93023.*"

I did not do this. I never wrote to the Magical Rainbow Man for my magic scroll and sticker. Even as a kid, I knew that this was taking it too far. This fact, and the fact that as an adult I now find this book to be funny, leads me back to the point of my story.

I connect with this way of looking at the world, but inevitably, at Some point, it loses me. It crosses a line that I can't define, or describe. And so, when I spend time with people who are deep into this perspective, on some level, I want to be a part of it, but I usually end up feeling like a fish out of water.

Part of the problem might be that there's not a lot of universal language that we can use to talk about spirituality. One person sharing their love for Christ can come across very differently from the yogi who experienced a deep bliss during savasana last night, even though they might be essentially talking about the same thing. It's hard to know where to meet people.

But I try. I go to events and gatherings and workshops, looking for my people, the ones I *will* connect with. But more and more it starts to feel like how I felt in gym class all throughout middle school and high school, where I failed at every sport, but then in the next semester, when we would get into something new, I'd think, "This is it. This is the one I'm going to be good at," or "I didn't think I was athletic, but then I tried pole vaulting!" And finally, I would have found my athletic calling. (Which never happened, by the way—finding my athletic calling.)

So with that same, perhaps naïve, optimism, I still seek out the occasional meditation class or spiritual workshop, looking for connection. Although not TOO many, because it turns out that transcendence is actually kind of expensive. And the classes start to blend together, too. I usually know before going in that a spiritual workshop will be led by a white lady from Kansas City, whose name is something like "Debbie Ravenfeather." Debbie is like, one-sixty-fourth Native American, and won't let you forget it. She has the dreamcatcher earrings with the long feathers that brush against the shoulder pads of her Kokopelli blazer, and after class she's selling her own line of designer sage bundles.

One of these workshops was particularly painful for me. It started out ok, when we did an "ecstatic dancing" exercise. It was set to deep jungle-electro-organic club music; the kind where there's a guy whispering in the background the whole time—*feel, soar, relax.* Kind of like a weird hippie rave, but without all the fun drugs.

50

But then "Debbie" led us through a guided meditation, and that's when things started to fall apart for me. First, we were supposed to pick our spirit animal. You might think would be easy, but I'm really indecisive and there are a lot of options. I've always loved squirrels, but we were going on this big journey into the outer galaxy to meet our star family, and I didn't know if a squirrel would be up to the job. What if the squirrel wanted to just hang out and eat nuts and take a nap? Which honestly sounded pretty good to me... But no! We had work to do here. Maybe I should choose a fox, or a dog. Or something that flies! What about a Pegasus? No, that was too much. I should just go with the fox. Foxes are cool, they're a lot like dogs AND cats. Also I should probably pack some snacks.

By this time, I'm already behind schedule. The rest of the group had begun their ascension, and I was left behind on the material plane, still packing my luggage and trying to remember what foxes eat.

Things didn't improve for me up in the stellar regions. I was becoming increasingly anxious about NOT finding my star family and, honestly, not having the kind of transcendental experience I had paid good money for. Meanwhile, my fellow travelers were having all kinds of amazing adventures—reuniting with lost loved ones, being greeted by celestial beings, and just having a groovy time on the astral plane. I knew that this was what they were doing because upon our return to earth, we were asked to share our experiences with the group. I sat silently as one person after another described their journeys, and asked questions like, "What does it mean that I met a figure clothed all in white, with a great halo around his head, beaming crystalline energy toward me?"

I didn't share my story of being late for the great lift-off, nor did I ask if squirrels can be reliable as spirit guides. No, I just sat and listened, and when it was over I went back into the patchouli-scented bathroom, and I actually cried, mourning the fact that, just like high school gym class, I had failed once again to find the thing I was good at, to find where I belonged.

It's true, I never did find my spiritual community, and that's still painful sometimes. But I have a lot of other ways I connect with people, and plus, my plants are really good listeners. I have practices that I enjoy and I can share those practices with other people, but I don't have to. I'm happy at home with my yoga mat and my crystals. And when I go to take a nap, I know my spirit squirrel will be right there with me.

When I met my partner three years ago, I fell completely in love and I fell hard. It was an experience I never really had before. Usually I took a more apathetic approach to dating. Before I met him, I was always working so hard on being successful in life that I didn't have time to think about becoming emotionally mature or worry about how to act in relationships.

To me, he was perfect; he seemed to love everything about me and the chemistry was amazing. It just felt like coming home. I used to joke that I thought he was a serial killer because it was too perfect. I was sure we were going to take the relationship escalator straight to blissville and never look back.

Looking back, I can also recall the terror I felt as well. But I played it cool—acted like I knew I was a catch and that I loved myself and all that shit. I mean, it wasn't totally disingenuous. I was busy measuring my worth externally and I was doing pretty well by society's standards. Well at least I *thought* I was, but something was always missing.

Secretly, I was counting down the days until he got bored or he saw the "real me" and it'd be over. I thought I'd even beat him to the punch and point out all the ways he seemed to prove that he didn't really want to be with me. No amount of reassuring would suffice. A year or so went by and it was still a mystery to me that I hadn't fucked it all up by now.

Since I'm a mental health therapist by trade, I like to *think* I have some very sophisticated psychological defense mechanisms and I know alllll the jargon to *sound* like I'm not an emotionally stunted 12-year-old pretending to be an adult. I mean, I was *literally* teaching classes on co-dependence and how not to project your shit on to other people. Meanwhile, I was not practicing what I was preaching.

I remember one day, at the inpatient drug rehab where I worked, I was running a group educating them about healthy relationships. We talked about loving yourself first, asking for what you need directly, and using "I statements." Then right after group, I ran to my phone to finish my epic text battle with my partner, saying:

**I feel** like **you** never make time for me…

**I feel** like **you're** so selfish and immature…

**I feel** like if you really loved me you'd show it by putting **my** needs first and rearrange all of your plans for me…

Then I went and cried in my office, wiped my tears and pulled myself together to go run another group. Then I'd come home, have a 4 hour fight with him and complain that he wasn't giving me enough quality time.

It's a mystery how I could be in **complete** denial of my own behavior and co-dependent tendencies. But denial is a pretty amazing thing actually, it's very comfortable. For a while…

You see, I thought all of our problems could be boiled down to one thing: he was not being a good partner and if he'd just change, then I'd be totally cool. Whelp, he disagreed. So we found a couples therapist and I was SURE she was going to scold him and tell me how right I was. Instead, she focused on me. She told me I had all these symptoms of co-dependency, that I was minimizing the impact of my "less than nurturing" childhood and, worse yet, I was being emotionally abusive, controlling and pushing my partner away.

I was like FUCK. THAT. I'm a therapist! I have my shit together. I help other people get their shit together. The real mystery is how this shit didn't get thrown in my face sooner.

We continued to go to therapy together for a while. We'd talk about the same stuff over and over. I'd defend my actions. We learned a couple new tricks to sound like we were making progress. And things did start to feel a *little* better. So what better way to throw more strain on a struggling relationship than to sign up for a week-long, intense road trip to the middle of the desert? What could possibly go wrong?

So, we bought tickets to Burning Man! I had never been before, my partner had been once, right before we met. If you don't know what it is, it's a week-long festival in the desert. I always thought it was just a big party, good dubstep music, lots of hippies doing lots of sex and drugs. And, don't get me wrong, it is all of that, but it's way more, too. It's also known to be really challenging both personally and on relationships. We joked to other people that we had to at least stay together long enough to make it to Burning Man. But behind the joke was a real fear that we wouldn't even make it one more week let alone the five months until Burning Man.

The next few months were very painful and confusing. We talked seriously about breaking up at least a dozen times. Things got so bad that my partner moved out of our room and into the spare room and we talked seriously about me moving out permanently. This went on for months. I was devastated. I felt abandoned and ashamed. I would come into his room begging him to move back into ours and when he'd refuse, I'd go cry myself to sleep.

We stopped seeing the therapist together but I continued on my own. And I went all in. A therapist in therapy, right? Soo meta! Somehow, things started to rapidly shift. In the midst of that chaos, I was starting to get more awareness; getting more hints at what I was really needing and wanting, but just trying to get in the most ass backwards of ways. I started to see that innocent, scared, wounded part of myself that needed a lot of love and support from ME. I actually put a picture of myself from one of the worst days of my childhood in a frame and I looked at her every morning and told her I was going to be there for her.

As Burning Man got closer and closer, things got worse and worse between my partner and me. Neither one of us was very excited to go to this intense event together. Less than a week beforehand, we considered selling our tickets and taking the $500 in camp fees we'd already contributed as a loss. For some unknown reason, we decided to go for it. I was prepared for the worst. I imagined he would abandon me, be off trying to have sex with all these beautiful festival girls (btw we're in an open relationship so that's not completely out of the question), and I'd be alone crying in our hexayurt for the majority of the week.

I asked myself if I could handle that and something told me I had to. I was so scared and confused, and then a strange thing happened; I just relaxed and surrendered. This didn't feel like a conscious choice: it was the only option left. There's a saying that "you don't get the burn you want, you get the burn you need" and I decided to see what that might be.

I think some credit should go to divine intervention. Like one night, a few days before we were to leave for Black Rock City, I came home and I was pissed at something so banal like he hadn't taken the trash out again. I started to go down the rabbit hole, thinking he is so disrespectful, he doesn't show me he loves me, no one ever considers me, etc. So I decided to take it out, you know, so I could throw it in his face later. On my way out, a giant purple dragonfly nearly hit me in my face. I believe in all that hooey stuff like animal totems so I rushed to look it up and it meant an "invitation for transformation". There was nothing left to do but surrender and trust. I said, oh well. This relationship might be over. And I'm still okay. It was lots of moments like that over time that led to a new understanding of my inherent self-worth. I accepted the invitation to transform.

And obviously, I survived! Actually, I did more than survive, I thrived! I've never had so much fun and felt so free! I was completely myself, my inner child was having a blast but my functional adult was on board to set limits, nurture myself and not get hooked into unhealthy relationship dynamics. Our relationship felt like how it did when we first met. We genuinely wanted to be around each other all the time. He even remarked on how much progress I've made in my recovery and how it scares him because now he knows it's his turn to work on his shit.

We've been back from Burning Man for about a month now. Since then, things have been a lot better with our relationship. I don't know, maybe it was the thousands of dollars of therapy I endured, or maybe it was the hundreds of hours I spent journaling and listening to self-help audio books. Or maybe it was an act of god or all the molly I did on the Playa. Who knows? It's a mystery. But something finally clicked. I feel like a completely different person. I've started to feel this really empowered, courageous, kind, and wise part of myself. Now, I feel THAT part of myself more than I ever have before.

There was this place at Burning Man that you could stick your head in this little hole and ask a fortune teller any question you had. I asked, "What does the future hold?" He responded with "It doesn't matter. Move along."

And you know what? He's right! Because now, I know no matter what happens, I have a good foundation of my own recovery and maturity to deal with anything. It feels so good, so exhilarating. Now I actually look forward to the unknown. I can't wait to see what mysterious shit will undoubtedly happen to me in my life. And for the first time, I feel more excitement than fear.

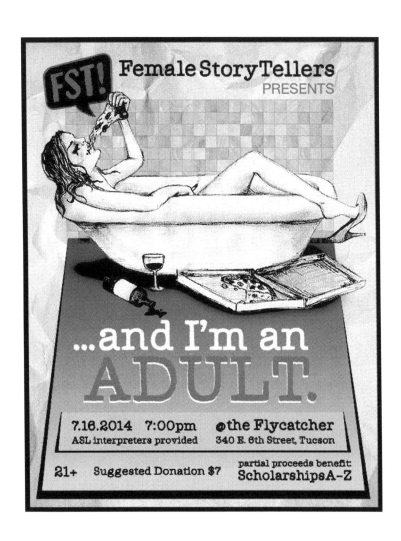

58

FST! Amanda Sierra
## "... And I'm an Adult" July 2014

When I started writing this, just for shits and giggles (and perhaps to further prompt myself out of a lingering writer's block), I looked up the definition of adulthood. It was rather bland on dictionary.com, but on Wikipedia there are apparently two types of adulthood: biological and legal.

For all intents and purposes, I am an adult. Legally, I can buy guns and purchase alcohol. I can buy porn and, if I so desired, I could even make it. I have a driver's license and I have not been financially dependent on my parents since I was seventeen. I've voted twice. Actually, I've voted once. I woke up too late and couldn't find my registration card for my first foray into democracy, so I just told everybody that I voted because they were being REALLY obnoxious about it that year. I think perfecting the "little white lie" may also be a marker for adulthood, but that's another FST! prompt entirely.

Biologically, I've been an adult since I turned thirteen despite the fact that my measurements are just past post-pubescent. I shed my uterine lining every month amid half-empty bottles of wine and Fleetwood Mac's "Silver Springs" on repeat. What is it about Stevie Nicks that makes menstruation/life okay?

So, I suppose you can say I landed somewhere in the realm of adulthood between the ages of seventeen and nineteen. What Wikipedia failed to mention were some very adult words that can also pertain to adulthood:

Pregnancy

Parenthood

Marriage

Divorce

I landed somewhere among all of those words in between the ages of nineteen and twenty-two.

At the age of nineteen, I thought I was rocking the shit out of adulthood. I had a used 2004 Hyundai I bought in cash from my job at the Marriott where I was about to roll into some sweet insurance options. I had a live-in boyfriend and we were starting to fight like real adults. I had found out bangs totally worked for me. When my mother called me, I said things were great. I was also becoming skilled in saying things were "great" or "okay" when they weren't.

I was carrying on just fine-ish until the summer of '07 came and I called her, in between tears and utter bewilderment, and told her things were not so great. Things were positive. I was pregnant.

The funny thing about unplanned pregnancies is that they very rarely come at a good time. You hardly ever hear of a story where a woman says "And then I found out I was pregnant and I was just totally cool with it and everything fell into place perfectly!" A thousand short stories, movies, and mommy blogs can't be wrong.

I spent the first week with the knowledge of my new interloper fluctuating between wanting to become a motherly goddess and crying in bed alone, telling myself "This can all go away. You still have time. You can still be in control of your life and get things back on track. You aren't ready to be a mother." And that was true. But as I stroked my formerly taut belly, I felt less alone. For the first time the previous suicidal thoughts and depression that had plagued my teenage years took a backseat to the fear and uncertainty that potential motherhood held. And those feelings were better. In the uncertainty, I found hope. When I asked myself, for the final time, "Do you want to keep this baby," I said "Yes," and that was true, too. I may have not been ready, but I was willing.

I went to a clinic and got my first look into what was going on inside the vessel that chaos seemed to surround. I saw a fetus floating around in the dark, upside down. I knew we were meant for each other in that moment. Two babies in a new upside down world.

I named him Jack.

Parenthood came easy for me. I love Jack with every fiber of my being and raising him has helped raise myself. Marriage, however, did not come easy. Jack's father and I had a turbulent relationship, despite wanting the best for all of us. All that adult-like fighting that was fine before I was pregnant, became tiresome during, and unbearable after. We were two entirely different people now. While he chased down promotions, I chased down a toddler and tried to figure out what I wanted to do once preschool started. I had put everything on hold to hold down the fort and be a good housewife. Eventually, resentment grew. The kind that flourishes between two people who look at each other and see themselves being held back from what they want out of the future.

As a child of two parents who should have gotten divorced long before I turned seventeen, I knew that we were producing a toxic environment. I didn't want Jack to eventually use his room as an escape fortress; retreating the second he got home with a knot in his stomach. I didn't want him to feel embarrassed at the idea of one day bringing friends over. I didn't want him to grow up thinking "This is normal." Or worse—"This is love." So I made the call.

I became a divorcee at the ripe ol' age of twenty-three. I moved in with my best friend and spent the next three years picking up the pieces while feeling like a complete failure. I had no degree to speak of (they don't exactly hand out Bachelor degrees for "Domestic Engineering"). I had dreamed of being a writer since I was in elementary school. So I did the next best thing that most English majors do after graduating: I became a bartender. I found out I truly loved it and things started looking up, but I still felt like I was a failure. I had done all of the adult things in such a short period of time. I had come out the other end alive even when things looked bleak. Why didn't I feel slightly more accomplished?

Every other week, I drive Jack up to school in Oro Valley. Men in ties drive their shiny SUV's to work and women with diamonds the size of my wisdom teeth on their ring fingers say goodbye to their children before shuffling off to their CrossFit classes. I pull up next them in my '96 Buick Century that my grandfather gave me before he passed. His final gift to the granddaughter he helped raise. I turn down the Black Sabbath so as to not to raise any eyebrows (and because Jack has asked me for the millionth time to turn it down) and I think "What am I doing here? I don't belong here." I didn't go to college and I'm not married and I don't have a mortgage. Jack's lunch for sure has gluten in it. I'm killing my child because I was a teen mother! BUT THEY SAID I WAS AN ADULT! THE WORLD TOLD ME I'M AN ADULT! I don't have a desk job and I cuss A LOT. Like, a lot. The phrase "Amanda, please don't say the word 'cunt' within earshot of guests" has been used by my coworkers and bosses. I hate cooking. I hate routine and planning for everything and talking about weddings and baby showers. When you're the product of a chaotic upbringing, these things seem foreign, without the intrigue of being foreign. I'm a damn bartender for Christ's sake. I go to bed when most people are jogging "for their health."

I pay for field trips, clothing, food, and after-school care with money that people give me in exchange for alcohol and conversation. But I DO pay for those things. That's part of being an adult, right?

And I work odd hours but I still read the bedtime stories and wake up ungodly early to take him to school (even if it means not going to bed at all sometimes). That's pretty adult right?

I am trying to raise a person into a functioning, compassionate human being (preferably with good taste in music and literature) while remaining true to myself and my goals. When he asks me questions about life I give him answers. That's adult as fuck.

Adulthood is not something you define in simple terms or through the random passing of time. It isn't a 401K or knowing what to claim on your taxes. Adulthood is taking your life in your own hands and unapologetically making it into something you are proud of. Adulthood isn't lying in bed and thinking about the what-ifs.

Last week, as I was dropping Jack off for his summer program, a child looked up from his drawing and sneered at me while hissing out a disdainful "Who are you?!" This happens a lot when you co-parent. Some people think Jack's stepmom is his real mother and I'm "The Help." Sometimes we all show up to events and sometimes maybe it's just me, or just his dad and stepmom. Sometimes my fiancée picks him up and sometimes my ex-husband picks him up. Oro Valley hasn't heard of divorce or if it has somebody ends up with a younger wife and somebody ends up with a timeshare in San Diego. I suppose it's hard to fathom that a person who works in engineering once impregnated somebody with visible tattoos and a penchant for tequila and the Velvet Underground. Usually, I go into a long-winded and awkward description of our family's status and my role in it. But why? I'M AN ADULT. Why do I have to explain myself after all of this? I didn't struggle to get to a place I finally feel happy in, only to apologize for it because it didn't fit into somebody else's idea of "adulthood."

I signed Jack in and kissed him goodbye before situating my sunglasses on my face. And I looked at the kid, still glaring at me and I said "I'm Jack's mom."

And I took a few steps toward the door, but not without letting out an audible-only-to-me "bitch."

Sometimes kids are dicks.

And sometimes, for all intents and purposes, I am an adult.

## "Luck Be a Lady" March 2016

Sex. We've had sex in private places, sex in public places, sex with strange faces, and sex in strange spaces. When we have gotten a little more adventurous, some of us have pulled it off (pun intended) successfully and some of us not-so-successfully. Here is a story of my not-so-successful time. I may share another one at a future date and figured I should warn you.

I dated a guy who named himself after an 80's hair metal dude, Vince, so this should have been my first red flag. Nope. I found him to be quirky and different. He was quirky because he nicknamed himself Ozzy because he loved Ozzy so much. He then watched The Matrix, and loved the band Tool, and started calling himself "Anima Trinity." Not even kidding. He also thought he was brilliant because he made up words like "componder" which is "comprehend" and "ponder" together.

Vince lived with his mom and never had a job that I know of. He said he would be a famous guitarist someday, but sucked at guitar. He thought he would meet Marilyn Manson or Maynard James Keenan from Tool and they would have this insane connection. He thought they would automatically understand one another at a level higher than most "average" people. He thought they would create music together. He didn't want to work so he could focus on his guitar playing. These are the things I tell myself so that I can feel better about my bad decisions.

The bad decisions were continuously dating men that "think outside the box" when really they wanted "open" relationships so they could do whatever they wanted. Most lived with their moms. One guy said he was in the middle of leaving his wife when he actually wasn't. Another guy I had a huge crush on told me I was like his sister after I gave him a blow job.

The attraction with Vince, to be honest, is that is he paid attention to me. I was very overweight (369 lbs). I was with someone, but was insecure. I needed to feel like someone else found me attractive. I didn't feel secure in my relationship because I was insanely insecure in myself.

He also had long hair and I thought long hair was cool. I just liked that he was attracted to me and he accepted me for my weight. These are, or were, my patterns of behavior. I so desperately wanted to be loved, and wanted men to be attracted to me, when I was so heavy. Any attention was attention, and I needed to feel like I mattered. Like I was pretty. Like I wasn't worthless because of how I looked.

We decided to go to the end of Speedway to make some sweet lovins, because he thought it was pretty and "romantic," even though he didn't have a car and I paid for the gas. Plus, he was a loser and lived with his mom, and I didn't want to go to my house and wake my parents up. I thought it would be fun to do something different and be kinky and rebellious.

When we got to the end of Speedway, we quickly started getting hot and heavy in my car. We both had our pants off and I am getting ready to position myself when I hear a noise. I asked Vince, "Did you hear that?" Vince of course says, "No. Keep going." Typical dude. Sorry, dudes, but you know it's true. So anyways, we continue making out and I hear the noise again and realize someone is driving up. I freak out and jump out of the car while Vince is in the car trying to put his pants back on. I'm running around and I can't find my pants anywhere. The car is approaching quickly so I run behind my car and guess who it was? Yep. You guessed right. TPD. So the cop gets out of the car, points his flashlight at me and asks, "Miss. What are you doing out here?"

Now I'm thinking, "Holy shit. I have no fucking pants on. He's a cop. What am I going to tell this cop? Mo. You're just going to have to come out with it. There's no other way." I take a deep breath in, shrug my shoulders put my hands up and say, "Officer. I was having sex and I don't have any pants on."

To my surprise, the officer got awkwardly uncomfortable and said,

65

"Well you need to gather your things, get in your car, and leave."

I said, "Of course, officer. No problem, officer." The officer then shines his light on some unidentifiable item which was hanging on a cactus and asks, "Is this yours?" And, in all honesty, I reply, "Could be." I mean, come on. I have no idea what the item was. I have no pants on so anything is possible at this point. The officer awkwardly says, "Ok. Well I am going to leave and I expect you to be out of here in the next 10 minutes."

He finally leaves and I take a deep breath and look at Vince and say, "Holy shit that was embarrassing but at least I didn't get arrested." Vince replies, "Should we go ahead and finish?"

I'm lucky because I didn't get in trouble and lucky because, later down the road, I learned to love and respect myself more. I'm worth more than a parking lot at the end of Speedway! At least the Motel 6, for fuck's sake! I kid, but really.

I lost weight and learned to feel more self-worth around who I am as a woman. I now work with victims of abuse and teach women about red flags, healthy vs. unhealthy relationships, and finding their own self-worth. I was also a victim and raised in an abusive home. In fact, 1 in 4 women are abused over the course of their lifetime, and that's just the ones who report it.

I'm so lucky to know what I know now and to stop making those mistakes. I am surrounded by beautiful women and we are fighting to have a voice and getting pretty good at it! Well, I still make mistakes every now and again. Okay. A lot. But we all do and that's what makes us human. Plus, if I didn't life would be pretty boring.

"A Letter to Anyone 2" May 2016

Dear Dad,

I haven't written to you for a very long time, though I know I wrote you letters even after you were gone. It's been almost fourteen years since I last saw you, and I miss you so much.

These past fourteen years have been so challenging. I'm not angry with you anymore. For a long time, I fought the demons you left behind, your inconsistencies, broken promises, manipulation, and your absences for months every year. I was and still am angry that my relationship with you was always trumped and defined by your alcoholism. What a true injustice that I did not get to know my real father without the poison.

After fourteen years, I know better, though. I know you fought a bitter war in your heart, and that you wrestled with self-loathing for years. I know you self-medicated, and I see now the pattern of your psychological breakdowns. I believe you slipped through the cracks because you sought help only in your manic cycle, and tricked the specialists into thinking you were capable of perpetuating your own recovery.

I worked with clients just like you; I found myself saying things to them I imagined someone saying to you in one of those halfway houses you lived in. I begged them to consider their families and friends, to take a minute to consider the people who cared for them who would be devastated by losing them. I can only hope I made any kind of difference.

In fourteen years, Dad, I've done so many things you would be proud of! I went to the University of Arizona, just like you wanted! I've traveled all over the United States, and visited Mexico and Canada, Japan, China, Thailand, and Malaysia. I lived in South Korea and taught beautiful Korean children to have conversations in English! I've painted pictures and taken photos and written prose about my experiences. I've worked with lots of animals and plants as a field biologist's assistant, and I've taught and tutored students at every age in a variety of subjects. I got my black belt in Tae Kwon Do! I have been in two belly dance troupes, on two separate sides of the planet! I've explored dozens of skills, broadened my horizons, and met thousands of amazing people. I think you'd be proud of all my experiences.

In fourteen years, Dad, I've turned into a badass cook—thanks to your inspiration! My friends love me for my sense of humor, which I certainly shared with you. I'm a walking encyclopedia, meticulous about facts, figures, and accuracy, and I thank you for my high standards. I love some really great music I think you would appreciate and enjoy. I took my GREs and got great scores! I worked for three years for my teaching certification, and I teach biology to high schoolers—they love me and I love them! Thank you for your love of learning, because I'm on fire with it and I delight in passing it along to my students. I'm gradually becoming a scientist, Dad, and I've got a research position this summer! I'm definitely making that long-awaited progress in my career path. I think if anyone in the whole family would have understood this part of my personality, it's you.

In fourteen years, I could really have used your advice with guys. I know you would have looked out for me if you were here. I've had my heart broken and shattered a few times—maybe I'm better for it, but the insight I gained so gradually over time all on my own could have been yours to share with me long ago. I've cried too long for the wrong men. I spent six of those years with a guy you met once, when I was 16 or 17. He reminded me of you so much, in good ways and bad. He was brilliant, charming, witty, sharp, sensitive, and a gourmet. He was also an addict, filled with self-hatred, bitter with his parents, emotionally distant, overweight, lazy, and a belligerent drunk. I let him keep me as far away as he possibly could, because I couldn't bear to lose the relationship, no matter how destructive. This is something you did to me: I was also accustomed to your emotional ebbs and flows—when you disappeared, I knew that a seven-page letter would preface your return. And then, you'd come back.

After fourteen years, Dad, I know you're not coming back. I have long since stopped having the dreams where you turned up, matter-of-factly, having 'just been down the street' all this time, neglecting to let me know. I haven't struggled with the lack of closure or goodbyes for a long time. I am not so haunted by the idea of dying alone in my apartment, only to be discovered days or weeks later. I've stopped picturing the grisly scene of your apartment after they found you, as Mom and I cleaned up your remaining possessions, and the evidence of your self-inflicted loneliness and despair. I can be by myself for long stretches, peacefully, without the anxiety of letting fragile, fickle friendships die. I'm actually quite vigilant in maintaining contact with my own friends who live alone, making sure they surface from time to time, and that they know I'm keeping tabs on them.

Dad, I do wish you could be here to share in my life. I don't really remember enough about you now to picture how you'd be in each scenario, though. My childhood was during your final spiral downward—how can I picture you in my life now? Would you guilt me about money or where I lived? Would you accuse me of abandoning you? Do you know how angry that made me? YOU abandoned ME. That's something I really can't picture having in my adult life. I don't think I could be there at your beck and call as a taxi service now, and I wouldn't have time to visit you at your halfway house, or in the hospital, or with the counselor who is clearly taking your side. I couldn't be the one responsible, not even PARTLY, for your sobriety. I couldn't accept that you just had no emotional maturity, and chalk it up to addiction and mental illness. I have no idea who you would be now. Would you be sober? Would you be healthy? Functioning? Would you have remarried? The Universe took you when it did for a reason. There was no future in the way you were living. You were dying.

I'm turning 34 this year, Dad. I'm kind of an adult, but I still struggle. The threat of hitting a "rock bottom" and ending up homeless feels very real to me. You being homeless so often has warped my faith in myself to survive. It is my worst-case scenario.

Also, in fourteen years, guess what? Mom and Richard are still married, and no, he never got a job. No, he never acknowledged sexually abusing your kids. No, Mom has never made him own up to it, or face any sort of consequence for it. They just pretend it didn't happen. Scott-free, right? So, you're all terrible parents. That should ameliorate some of your fatherly guilt. I was thoroughly intimidated by the prospect of having my own kids, and following any of my examples of parenting growing up.

I'm not so intimidated now, Dad. I have spent so much time, effort, and money on healing and finding myself. I'm pretty stable, centered, mature, and emotionally available. I know my best self and I try to prioritize that strong woman I know myself to be. I am so much better at knowing how not to put up with bullshit; I can spot it sooner and react quicker. I'm much more skilled at identifying and exercising my boundaries in relationships, and I don't suffer any fool, let alone an abuser, or a fucking addict, or a belligerent drunk. I feel much more open and capable of giving and receiving love, real love that connects people at their souls. I think I could even manage an honest-to-god healthy, long-term relationship, and maybe even have a family that I won't fuck up with volatile insecurities. I think I could be a consistent and supportive member of this family, and still be honest about my humanity.

Remember, Dad—you used to send me the Letter, always just addressed to me, even though the whole family wondered where you were and what the hell happened. I sat down and read that Letter, each time it came, and you always accused me of not caring what had happened to you, or what you'd been doing for the 6-plus months you'd been off the map. You know that shit was completely unfair. You were embarrassed of YOURSELF— I was never embarrassed of you. I always cared. I always waited; I always called. I even took your side, a LOT.

But, you know, after fourteen years, I've made my peace that you're gone. I know you were living an unsustainable, shaky life, and I can find solace that you were freed of your suffering. I don't fight so many of those demons anymore. So this is me writing YOU a Letter now. Pages and pages of what I've been up to for fourteen years, and

I know you care, and I know you would have wanted to be there for these things. I miss you Dad, and I always will.

Your loving daughter,
 Amanda

FST! Female StoryTellers presents:

# Secret Identities

Proceeds Benefit:

"ALLY"

A SAAF Program

Suggested $7 donation (cash only)

Wednesday, October 30th, 2013
7:30 PM
(doors at 7 PM)

PLUSH
340 E 6th St, Tucson, AZ

ASL Interpreters provided    Facebook.com/FStoryTellers

**FST!** Benjamin Z. Griffith
"Secret Identity" October 2013

'Evening, folks.

So, why is there a man here on stage at an event specifically called "Female Storytellers"? Well, as some of you know, the theme tonight is regarding secret identities, and I, myself, have one. And it's because of this secret identity that I am sharing my story with y'all tonight, because my secret identity is that I was actually born as a female. That may or may not have some folks going through a head spin right now. Kind of the story of my life these days. Half the time, this part of my identity is such a secret, not because I actually want to hide it from everyone else, but because I am so aware of it that I'm not used to being read as male yet.

I'm sure it puzzles some—how I could forget that I'm a guy... who was born female? Let me rewind a little bit.

So, yes, I was born female. And, I lived my life—or attempted to live it—as female up until a few weeks after I turned twenty-one. Twenty-one—that's usually an exciting age, isn't it? You get to vote, you get to drink, you get to gamble, and, in my case, you get to discover your true identity. In a way, I had won the lottery—I had figured out my true identity, or at least the start of it, as being transgender. On the other hand, it was still a gamble, and all I had was a new hand to play.

Because being trans does kind of start off as a secret identity. Like your favorite superhero, there's the change of wardrobe and an alias name to suit the secret identity, and the regular clothes and name to suit the "normal" one. My case was a little bit unique. See, I was already dressing the part—I had come out as a butch lesbian about a month or two before I came out as trans. However, that never settled well with me. Mainly because of these. Right, I forgot—you can't see them. Oh, they're there, trust me. But, that's the beauty of binding, see? My breasts become Ninja Tits. Take the binder off, not amusing. Put the binder on and voila! Poof! It's a brand. New. Chest! You have

73

no diaphragm and hardly any air, but the girls are down and that's all that counts. You get used to it after eight years.

So, as some of you are gathering, transitioning has its pains. It's a transformation of my body in two ways—via the presentation and the binding, and then via medical means. One is more readily available than the other, or else I could just lift my shirt and show y'all the scars of the Ninja Tits' last showdown. But it's not just a body transformation. This is where the secret identity, or double life, comes in.

One of the greatest banes of transitioning is the waiting period. Waiting to get everything aligned: the body, the gender marker, the name. For seven years, I was going by two different names—my preferred name with my friends and chosen family, and my given name for the sake of legalities, like when I was doing business at a bank, or registering for classes. Let me tell you, that can be tedious—and embarrassing, at times. The first couple of years, I was being read as more female than male, despite my presentation. The next few years after that, I would be read as male until I opened my mouth.

These last two years, since taking testosterone shots, I am fully read as male pretty much most of the time—which is great, but then I hear girls commiserate over their time of the month and tell 'em, "Oh, I feel your pain. My own time of the month was a bitch!" And then they go, "Um, what?" Oh yeah... "So let me back up. I'm trans... " Thankfully, this takes place with friends of friends. I don't know why I automatically assume that just because my friends know that I'm trans, their friends would know, too.

So it's also possible that some may be wondering, why would I transition just to tell my story on a female-only stage? And since I'm pretty much out anyway, how is my trans* identity a secret one? Because as I've said, I'm mostly read as male now—and yet, I don't forget where I came from. Some who transition choose to live stealthily and totally disengage from that part of their past. And that's their prerogative. I, however, choose not to. I choose not to, not just because I can empathize with other women regarding the pains of the monthly cycle (though I'm sure girls can appreciate a man who actually knows how it is). But, no. I choose not to forget my herstory, as it were, because it holds me accountable. How does it do that? Because transitioning from female to male has its pros and its cons, and one of the cons is stepping into male privilege.

But how in the world could privilege of any sort be such a bad thing? Oh, I don't know. Have you seen Congress lately? I mean... just sayin'.

But yeah, I choose to be out as a way of holding myself accountable in spaces of privilege, including those that do help, as a way of keeping myself protected, such as when I choose to walk home late at night, or go out and party in a club. And in those situations, I also can be the extra eye that knows what to look out for with others— especially with regard to women who are dealing with misogyny and patriarchal bullshit from guys who just don't get it. You know the ones. P!nk dedicated one of her top hits to them. ("U + Ur Hand", it was called). As a way to keep myself in check so I don't become one of those guys (and if I do, slap it outta me), I choose to identify as a trans man instead of as just a man. Because in my mind, I am kind of a liaison between two binary genders. Even though I am out, I've got one foot in each world, and my body reflects this externally. Well, beneath the clothes anyway.

And it's true. In a lot of ways, my mindset is still female-oriented. But in some ways, I kind of get where the guys are coming from, too. And yet, I still can't completely understand either one of them half the time!

So, it will always be a double life. And, it's a secret identity by the main fact that you just can't tell by looking at me. But unlike most secret identities, it's not a mask or a separate ID card. For the most part, I'm hidden in plain sight—kind of like the cast of Touched By An Angel. The concept of interacting with someone who might just end up being something you weren't expecting, and yet they touch your life and open your eyes—that's what I'd like to be for people. And that's the gift in my secret identity.

# FST! Leigh Spencer
## "Parents Just Don't Understand" June 2016

Hi. My name is Leigh. I live in Arizona. And I'm FAT.

If you were to ask my mother, she'd tell you that's all you really need to know about me.

In fact, that's pretty much exactly what she tells her friends. I know this because one of them was really surprised, upon meeting me, to find out there was more to the story. She told my mom, "Rachel! You never said your daughter was an author or such a talented baker. Did you know she's an event planner? All you said is that she lives in the middle of nowhere in some desert and that she has two boys and a weight problem." She assured me that I was lovely and that, if I were her daughter, she'd be bragging to people about me.

I deflected with a joke about adoption possibilities. My mom looked the other way.

I was a fat kid, too. A more neutral outsider might say I was a little chubby. But my mom knew better. Long before we ever had to buy my Garanimals in husky sizes, my mom knew I was FAT and that that was the absolute worst thing in the world that I could be.

She tried to feed me sandwiches without the bread. She tried to sprinkle grapefruit halves with the evil bitterness that is Sweet 'N Low and call it breakfast. When I wanted a grilled cheese, she'd broil some cottage cheese on a single slice of toast. She took me to a pediatrician who told her to only feed me dinner two or three nights a week. I was six years old.

See, my mom USED to be fat. As a kid and through most of her teenage years. Since her parents had been nearly starved to death in German concentration camps, coming to America to start a new, prosperous life with a very chubby, obviously well-fed toddler was kind of a perfect "FUCK YOU, we made it!" to the Nazis. It was a badge of honor. Until it wasn't.

About the time my mom was ready to go to college, my grandparents had the epiphany that they'd need to get her married off pretty soon and that her prospects would be very slim if she were not.

Before Weight Watchers and healthy eating tips—like that really helpful cottage cheese monstrosity that looked like broiled vomit on toast—doctors in the early 60's had a different, more effective methodology. Prescription speed. True to its name, it worked FAST. The day my mom married my dad, she weighed less than 90 pounds.

She never gained it back. She had plenty of arguments with my stepdad over how skinny she was and how little she was eating, especially when she would do things like test pasta for doneness and spit the chewed noodle out to avoid the calories and then eat a slice of dry toast for dinner while we ate baked ziti. She catered to my stepdad in pretty much every way, but this was one area that was all hers to control. She ran a tight ship, fueled by cigarettes and diet Fresca and held together with sugar free gum.

So imagine what an epic BUMMER, what a visible FAILURE it was to have a FAT daughter. She couldn't get me speed because doctors weren't really doing that anymore, especially not for little kids. She did what she thought would be the next best thing. Ballet lessons! We had a studio, Mary Lou Hale's School of Dance, that was walking distance from our apartment, so she wouldn't even have to drive my latchkey ass there. All little girls dream of being graceful, swan-like ballerinas in pretty pink tutus and sparkly sequins, right? WRONG. My dream was to have a pet iguana. But, because it would be great exercise and because being around thin, pretty girls would motivate me, I got a year's worth of ballet lessons. Happy birthday to me.

I HATED ballet. I was short, stubby, and supremely unathletic with poor hand-eye coordination thrown in for good measure. Ballet was grace, elegance, tight pony tails, and discipline. I was the antithesis. I couldn't even reach the practice bar properly. The teacher didn't know what to do with me. She tactfully told my mom I might be more suited to tap. You know, the dance you'd be better at if stomping around like a baby hippo was more your style. But those shoes were expensive and the tutu was already paid for, so goddamn it, I was going to be a ballerina.

I made it through one performance. The teacher stood me in the back, think far, far outfield, and told me to just kind of sway along with the music. After the show, I couldn't get my leotard off fast enough and I peed all over my tutu. Thus ended my dancing career. I wonder if mom got her money back for the rest of the year?

She tried other stuff. Forbidding afternoon snacks for me, while providing them for any of my friends who came over to play. Counting all the cookies or chips in the house to make sure I hadn't taken any. Cutting lines in the ice cream carton so she could monitor the levels and make sure none went unaccounted for. And my all-time favorite—not calling me down for cake at my own fucking birthday party. If we had an MRI machine here, I bet you could still see the scar from that one.

Then there were the fad diets. I remember one time, I had to take these fiber pills that looked honest-to-God exactly like rabbit turds. I took twelve of them with three or four glasses of water before each meal to try to decrease my appetite. I guess they are supposed to expand in your stomach and take up all the space where food should go. Mom could never figure out why they didn't work for me. I dunno. Metabolism is a funny, tricky thing. Or it could be because I would take the pills, eat a few small bites of dinner, and claim to be full to make her happy. Then, later that night, I'd sneak eat the entire Entenmann's cheese danish I had hidden under my bed that I bought with money I stole from her purse. Who can say?

When I was a teenager, desperate times called for desperate measures. She switched gears from thinly veiled health concerns to more blatant shaming techniques. Back to school shopping became the stuff of nightmares. Open pen-style dressing rooms with mirrors on all sides and my mom, making sure everyone in there knew that we'd be buying whatever fit because nice clothes that I actually liked would be my reward for losing weight. In her defense, plus sized fashion has come a LONG way since then, so the options for size 14 me would have been limited. But in MY defense, she still didn't have to be such a BITCH about it.

By the time I was 17, there wasn't even the slightest pretext that she was concerned for my health anymore. My mom suggested that I start smoking and even offered to pay for my cigarettes because they might dull my taste buds, make food less yummy, and give me something non-caloric to do with my mouth. Which I already had boyfriends for, but whatever. I was born with asthma and endured many visits to the ER every single New Jersey winter because my lungs suck and I couldn't breathe. I could not believe what she was suggesting. I asked her if she'd rather have me thin and dead. She didn't respond right away. Not because what I said shocked or hurt her, but because she had to fucking think about it. She told me that the thing that would disappoint her most was if I stayed fat my whole life.

And there it was. Out loud. Something I suspected, probably knew, all along.

I always had this idea, back when gaining her approval was more important than it is now, that I could get her to see past this. All I had to do was somehow make my achievements bigger than my ass.

I got the lead in my school play. She asked if anyone else auditioned.

My choir was chosen to sing at Carnegie Hall. I repeat—I was onstage at CARNEGIE FUCKING HALL. She opted not to go because classical music wasn't her thing.

I had my first child. She accused me of having a boy to spite her because she really wanted a granddaughter.

I had my second son. (Take THAT, Mommy Dearest!) She couldn't figure out why. Why would I want TWO kids? What I was trying to prove? Also? She thinks the names I picked out for them are ugly.

After my first book came out (which she called my "little pamphlet"), I came in third place for best local author in Tucson Weekly's 2014 Best of Tucson. HOLY SHIT, right? J.A. Jance won first place and my mom makes it a point to mention how much she enjoys her novels almost every time we speak.

None of it mattered. Me + Fat = perpetual, disappointing, fuck up. Always and no matter what. This was how she viewed the world and I think her perceptions trapped us both. For self-preservation, I started holding my cards closer to my chest. I never told her how many months of fertility treatments we went through to have that second son that I wanted so desperately, even though I had nothing to prove. I didn't tell her about his birth defect either, until we sent a family portrait and I thought I should tell her, rather than just pretend we didn't notice. (Although that was SO tempting. "Oh my god! What's wrong with the baby's face?" "I dunno. He looks okay to us.") I never told her that I had a second book published.

Maybe she'd be able to see all of this as the success story that I KNOW it is if it had been accomplished by her imaginary size 4 daughter instead of her real size 24 daughter. She spent so much time focusing on a surface she couldn't change, she missed out on all the really important stuff underneath.

I don't hate my mother. I've just learned to meet her where she is. She's really, inappropriately funny and I love that I share her nasty sense of humor. When she freaks out and tells me what a bad mother she was, I let her off the hook. Whatever she did or didn't do helped make me the person I am now, which I'm gonna say deserves some love and gratitude, because I'm pretty cool.

We all have demons—some fat, some thin. At the heart of it all, she was trying to help me. I really think she did the best she could, the only way she knew how.

She thinks the reason we don't have a better, closer relationship is on me, because I'm so busy—like Harry Chapin, Cats in the Cradle style. I let her keep thinking that. It's kinder than the truth and the past is gone anyway. If I introduced myself now, as the daughter she really doesn't know; if I told her that I'm truly happy and I love my life, fat ass and all; if I let go of all the anger, regret, and hopes for what our relationship should have been; if I held her accountable and if forgave her, she wouldn't understand.

So we'll just leave things as they are. Keep it simple: My name is Leigh. I live in Arizona. And I'm FAT.

FST! Female StoryTellers present:

# There's no Place Like Home

Featuring special guest
storytellers from LA:

**TJ Huberg**
(Comedian / Storyteller)

**Myriam Gurba**
(Writer / Storyteller)

**FRIDAY, JUNE 21**
**7:30 PM**
(Doors: 7pm)

**LoveSmack**
**Studios**
19 E. Toole
Tucson, AZ 85701

**$7**
(suggested donation,
cash only)

*ASL Interpreters
will be available!

facebook.com/FStoryTellers

# FST! Lauren Wiggins
## "There's No Place Like Home" June 2013

Some people actually grow up in Arizona but many are transplants; for instance, it only takes about three beers for my Southern drawl to betray me. And in each "darlin'" and "y'all" you can almost hear the summers I spent traipsing through the sand dunes of Folly beach. You can feel your toes in the pluff-mud and see the marsh sway in my voice, and you know that South Carolina is the place I call home. But, after living there for 23 years, home never felt so much like home until I was leaving. And at the same time, the months leading up to my cross-country move to Tucson, home felt like being on some distant planet, playing Russian roulette with my air supply.

Now, pay close attention, because a lot of shit happened in the spring months before I graduated and moved. Here are some condensed highlights:

1. I freaked out about getting a job and began to realize that I didn't even know what I was qualified to do with a Bachelor of Arts in Women's & Gender Studies and a cognate in Sexuality & Representation. After all, I was only using my major as a pick up line.

2. I desperately needed to escape the oppressive humidity of the South and the bit of bigotry that occurs in some areas.

3. I enlisted in Americorps. If you don't know what that is, it means I'm a hero in America.

4. I went through a very nasty break up that left me without a roommate and short on rent.

5. My Mom was evicted from her apartment and moved into my place.

Article a. She was dating a crackhead named Brad, who moved into my place with her.

Article b. When I say that Brad was a crackhead, I mean that he enjoyed a myriad of drugs but he was most fond of dirty, nasty, filthy crack.

6. I fell in love with a gal from work who was also enlisted in Americorps.

7. We decided to find Americorps jobs out west. Because, fuck the north.

Now that you have some background, fast forward to May, when Mommy and Brad moved in with a millionaire (that's a whole different story) and I moved into the corner of a friend's living room. I had been at that apartment for two years and had acquired many things.

Basically, moving just meant throwing away a bunch of shit: a family couch I had been sitting on for 20 years, a wine bottle collection (some of the best $10-$15 bottles), some steel toe Durango work boots that my father left behind the second time he walked out of my life. There were ill-gotten street signs, and naturally, a pile of wood that I had convinced myself I would build stuff with when I drunkenly discovered it on the side of the road.

Anyway, I sold a bunch of my outlandish thrift store purchases to a drag king, like ya do; it was mostly blazers and checkered pants from the 70s. Once I condensed all my belongings down to a twin bed, some awesome t-shirts that no one will ever make get rid of, and my dog, I moved into my homeboy Juice's house. It shouldn't surprise you that I have a friend named "Juice." The deal was to pay one electric bill and make a Lauren nook in the corner of his living room ("Lauren Nook": SEE ALSO: aforementioned twin bed, on the floor – no box spring, two real walls and two fake walls - a bookshelf and a couch end).

By mid-July, I was narrowing down Americorps positions to Tucson and Phoenix and I had saved up a few hundred bucks. It was at this time that I moved, again, down to my Uncle Tom's, where he had some work for me to do for the rest of the summer.

Uncle Tom told me he'd give me a grand to one-woman-wrecking-crew a property he had recently acquired, 561 Savannah Hwy. It was an old Charleston home in the historic Byrnes-Down neighborhood, which was an area that was becoming highly commercial.

What you should know and is vital to this story is that this house, which had gradually begun to crumble over the recent years of vacancy, was my Aunt Brenda's house. And since she moved into that place in the early 80s, it was the center of all of our family Christmas parties, Thanksgivings and New Year's celebrations. It was decked out in some really great antique furniture like the velvet Victorian couches that my Grandmere saved up for and would proudly announce "paid cash."

All the kids knew better than to touch any of Auntie Bren's vintage knick-knacks, and 561 Savannah Hwy was thought to be our young family's collective home. In fact, almost all of my family members lived in the upstairs apartment at one point or another. My Mommy, my brother and myself lived there on two separate occasions. Yeah, both times I had to share a room with my little brother and, the second time, I was just learning the joys of menstruation, so that wasn't fun for both parties.

Something else you should know: my Aunt Bren had taken to hoarding clearance items, usually seasonal stuffed animals and trinkets she bought at the corner drug store. She also had an impressive collection of old patient charts from when she was a phlebotomist. I would later discover that this was called a "HIPAA violation." So, even though this place was slated to be rented to a group of lawyers and had just been gutted, my aunt's attachment to the remaining random shit inside was slowing down the money train.

Auntie Bren had collected so much crazy shit that, honestly, for the first week, I wasn't even present of mind. As I cleared the remaining debris, I looked past the exposed beams where walls used to hold laughter, not even thinking about the old watercolor prints of the

Charleston Market that used to hang there. Nope, I mostly stood to the side and patiently waited as my aunt looked over her things the way a gambler does the last of their chips, slowly pushing one more piece to the spot where it would be unceremoniously taken away. Then, once I was given permission, I'd take another truck load of unused gift bags and teddy bears wearing Santa hats to the Goodwill down the road.

Oh, and I mowed the shit out of that lawn. And I edged the driveway and shaped the hedges. My Grandmere was there with us for a few of those days, overseeing the project, and told me I had done a beautiful job.

Toward the end of August, I was going over to the house on my own more, mainly removing remnants from an unfinished, finished garage project that my Aunt Bren had once earnestly embarked on. Hey, guess what was in there—you guessed it, bags of stuffed animals holding hearts and shit.

During those last days, I also got to employ the use of an axe and a sledgehammer to destroy a fairly rotten privacy fence, which was my favorite part of the whole deal, because: sledgehammer.

So up until this point, everything was all about purging materials— the couch, the wine bottles, and the boots had only been the beginning. Then, it was watching my aunt get rid of all the shit that the rest of us didn't see the value in keeping.

Aside: OH MY GOD, the medical supplies. Quick poll: Have you ever tried to move a hospital bed through a house with doorways that were built in the 1920s? If the answer is "no," my advice is to pay a couple of strapping young men, or a nice lady who does CrossFit or ROLLER DERBY, $20 each to do it for
you.

Fast forward to my very last trip to 561 Savannah Hwy. I was gathering up my tools and there were a few spare items like a microwave, some folding chairs, a couple dishes, and the ashes of our beloved Siberian Husky, Mushka.

It was my final trip, so I decided to honor this place that I had called home in the most appropriate way a thug like myself knows: I smoked a big fat blunt to the dome.

About 20 minutes later, after my "commemoration ceremony," I got nostalgic and I began thinking about the finite things and the deliberateness of life.

My inner monologue said "Dude, you're moving 2,000 miles away from here."

And then I was all, "I know, right!?!"

Then I thought, "That's crazy, man."

And then I was like, "Where'd I put that commemorative beef jerky snack?"

So, here I am in the midst of some truly heavy contemplation when I suddenly became fixated, staring at a pile of more random shit that I'd left next to the front door for loading. One of the things awaiting transport was an old, blue china vase that had lived on the fireplace mantel before I was even tall enough to know it was there. Next to it was the ugly, plastic, tower canister containing Mushka. It was then that I had the best idea ever!

I carefully transferred Mushka to the china vase and was pleased with the perfect fit. I also lovingly taped the top of the china vase to ensure Mushka's safe travel. Then, I set it on one of those exposed beams I mentioned, stepped back to admire my work and turned to finish loading the truck.

Finally, I did the obligatory once over: checked closets and corners for anything I might have forgotten. I even did a run through of the upstairs apartment, and when I descended, I spared no expense in closing the door at the bottom of the stairwell, in the fashion it had always favored—I slammed that motherfucker shut as hard as I could. In that exact moment, so many things ran through me; things that had

87

been apparent but were nowhere near as processed as that delightful beef jerky. Wouldn't ya know, just when I had finally gotten the hang of it, this would be the very last time I slammed that door, and that privacy fence that had kept a tinier version of me from wandering into traffic was done, son. At this moment, I also became aware of the crash in the next room.

When I peeked around the corner to confirm the fear that my faithful family dog of fourteen years was indeed, all over the floor, I realized that I wasn't quite as "done" with South Carolina as I thought.

Of course, I put Mushka back in the ugly, plastic canister and told absolutely no one what happened, but as I swept her up, I cried. It had been the first time I had allowed myself to cry about anything since February—since I got rid of my dad's boots, since I said goodbye to everyone I had come to know and love in college, since I watched my Mom really go off the deep end.

Truth is, while separating pieces of two things I had grown up with: Mushka and the vase, I did allow myself a good, honest, QUICK! nobody-is-watching cry, as I cleaned up the last mess I would ever make in that house. And maybe I did grow, even as I left the driveway, because when I think about that moment today, I no longer try to "remember what I came from so I never have to go back." Instead, when I visit and have to remind my Mom that "I'M GOING BACK TO TUCSON," I can't help but believe that going home isn't a thing you should deny yourself.

# Part 2: Purpose
## *What We Do*

One aspect of storytelling that always strikes me as truly life-altering is that it provides a framework of self-authorship. Our lives become more than just the circumstances we've been born into or the events that have occurred to us as we've grown. We start to recognize the things we can't change, as well as the things we can—and as we develop the wisdom to know the difference, we become autonomous actors in the drama of our lives, making choices and taking strides in the direction we decide to lead ourselves.

## FST! Anna Stokes
## "Bad Reputation" September 2016

I have a confession: I am a Christian single lady who has sex. Now, don't be alarmed, I already know I'm like this cultural chimera. The sex thing showed roots back when I was eleven: hormones happened, I went boy-crazy, and I have never returned. Really, though, sex was on my brain even before boys were. My mom says it was par for the course for me to explore masturbation as a kiddo. (I don't remember that at all, but I believe her.) Long before I could identify the feeling of arousal, I had these past-bedtime fantasies about Kaa—the snake from the animated Jungle Book, specifically where he'd hypnotize and kidnap women, disrobe them, and... just... constrict them. You don't have to say anything; I know it's fucking weird. But when you're a kid, you can't explain what floats your boat, you just know that you're buoyant.

My luck with human men in the real world has been tragicomically underwhelming. This is in spite of the fact that I fall in love with just about every other man I meet or see: the married retiree with the Antonio Banderas voice (and charm) who came into my work the other day; the Fry's cashier who asked me on a cemetery first date (though to my credit, I did say no); the lumberjack bouncer at the Flycatcher... Yeah, I said it. [Author's note: FST! performs at Flycatcher. Said bouncer wasn't there that night, but he heard about the mention, and we later met at Tucson Hop Shop and I totally admitted my crush to him. Whoopsy-daisy.]

In college, I did some good mental grappling with whether I'd consider sex before marriage. I was a student leader in this campus Christian group and, at the time, I felt like a bad Christian because I swore, smoked occasionally, and drank underage. (Sidebar: now I don't give a shit. Cheers!) The Christian club's pastoral figure was my friend and mentor, Caleb, this total wild-man philosopher. He loved to call people out, and he sure did with me my senior year, when I told him I'd had my first kiss.

The kiss (okay, makeout sesh) in question, long overdue in my mind, was worth the wait: New Year's Eve, in a dive bar in Greenwich Village, with a New York Italian bartender from Long Island. Caleb warned me that frenching would ultimately lead to sex. At the time I was like, "Lol, please."

Maybe a year and a half later, I realized: "Oh shit, dude was right." I was housesitting for my godparents and this guy came home with me. It was the first time I'd been naked with a man (at the time, I felt too awkward to fully look at him), and my first time giving and receiving oral. Early in the evening, I made the mistake of texting my mom—who also happens to be a pastor's wife—that the guy was hanging out. (I am a TMI queen, okay? Also I wasn't into the idea of him murdering me, or at least getting away with it.) He spends the night, and around 8:30 in the morning, there's a knock at the door. "Hide!" I yell, throwing on pants. Lo and behold, it's my concerned, well-meaning parents, who want to come in and comfort and chide me while a naked dude is holding his breath in the master bathroom.

When I looked at my phone about an hour before this most embarrassing moment of my life, I saw a text from my mom, something along the lines of, "Honey, I'm worried," capped by an ominous ellipses. Reality washed in again, and I sank. I didn't feel bad at all about fooling around the night before—it was one big scary thrill—until I thought of my context.

The thoughts that entered my brain after Mom's text were totally irrational. I pictured this majorly judgmental church that just isn't mine. I was like, "Am I gonna have to go up in front of the congregation and announce that I had a dick in my mouth!?" The American Christian sex and morality complex had been living in me, and it took that opportunity to explode into Fear.

That emotional whiplash took its time peacing out. My fears of rejection and shame were deeply misplaced—and no, I never had to atone publicly in front of my church; my folks didn't fucking want that. Only a few of my Christian friends know that story, and they've had sex sans-marriage, too. But there was real sadness wrapped up in my panic, because I care about the true family that my church has always been for me. Maybe this is misguided and patriarchal, but I did feel, sharply, how my use of my own body could potentially impact, and even sadden, those I love.

Without wanting to, I began to feel the divide between my church self and my sex self, because I just wasn't gonna quit those mediocre flings. There was a season when I wondered if one night stands with complete strangers—as in, don't buy you a drink first, meet them at their house strangers—might be for me. That question got answered in the most awkward way possible. I matched with some guy on Tinder, and he sent me the boring "Hey Anna, how's it going?" message. Obviously I didn't answer. But then he sends this veritable novella detailing what he'll do to please me sexually, culminating in the best—and most—orgasms of my entire life. Like, I guess he could see into the future? Like some kind of vagina prophet?

I decide to message back, in like a totally low key way. But of course, next thing I know he's asking if I can have him over, and I'm like, "Lol, nope, I live with my parents." Turns out that he lives with his friend and her mom, but then he starts backpedaling about how the friend's in Phoenix today and the mom is like, relegated to the first floor so it's no prob. I text my friend Angela—who I routinely talk about sex and hookups with—fill her in on the sitch, and ask, "Should I go for it?" And she's like, "DEAR GOD NO!" But then I'm like, "Is it terrible I'm considering? The mom is quiet and the walls are thick!" and she says, "You know what, go for it. I have to hear this story."

When I get to the guy's house, it turns out he's shy. The same orgasm oracle who wrote me erotica is small-talking with me on his bed, afraid to make the first move. Even when things do heat up, he's still quiet. I have to cajole him into sex talk. I whisper, "What do you want to do to me?" and he's like, "I wanna fuck you." Plain as white bread. So I tell him to take control, and he tells me to go down.

Now, I feel good about my blowjob game, but I do have a strong gag reflex. Maybe two minutes in, I choke and have to pull off, and at the same moment, he unleashes a straight-up Old Faithful of sperm.

Which gets everywhere, by the way. Cut to me feeling awkward, and him getting all enigmatic, which starts to freak me out. But, no matter, after a few minutes he's back in the saddle. Again, I try talking dirty: "Does it feel good being inside of me?" He goes, "Yeah." That's all I get?! Major side-eye over here.

See, prior to this, I'd been with dudes who were liberal with their compliments and vocal with their desires. In this moment, I'm shaken, and it only gets worse when he rams into my cervix. He's behind me and can't tell that he hurt me, so I have to say so, and we pause. And get back at it… until he does it again. I pull away, shaking my head no, and start to cry. In front of this shy, naked stranger who has absolutely no idea what to do with me. It's like when you come across some animal in the wild and throw each other for a mutual loop.

(Though let's be real, he was tame; I was the wild one.)

So yeah, that ended well. But really, it kind of did because on the drive home, I actually felt happy, and a little lighter. I had my answer on one night stands, and I thanked God for that; plus I wasn't, like, enslaved in his basement, and dude used a condom without being asked. So far, I've had a range of sex—the good, the bad, the kinky— but it's only ever been casual. It's definitely not the best thing in the world when you don't really know, or maybe even care about, your partner. At its best, casual sex is as good as yoga, because both bring me into the present. It feels about as good as chocolate tastes. It's not better than In 'n' Out animal fries, or a really hearty laugh, or a solid prayer time. And in these casual encounters, the things I long for have eluded me: love, connection, commitment.

I have never felt like God is wagging their finger at me. Once, when praying, I thought: "It must be time to deal with the sex thing by now. To feel like I have to give it up already." And I felt God say, with great tenderness, "One thing at a time." Which gives you an idea of how big my mess is. (Don't get me wrong; I love my mess.)

I had this vivid picture once, after the post-sex parental ambush, of myself in my godparents' hallway with Jesus. He was standing in front of me, smiling down, eyes warm, holding my shoulders in his

94

hands. I was there in my t-shirt and underwear, braless. (Not in, like, a cute way; in a sleep-deprived, kinda-have-to-poop way.) All he said was, "You're beautiful." And I cried, for real, because that's what I've been wanting to hear all along.

I am proud of my complex identity, of my sexual and spiritual selves, together, in tension, in conversation. One time in San Francisco, a car full of women about my age pulled over to ask if I was going to see the fight—I guess there was some MMA thing at a bar in the area.

And I said no, I was going to church. One of them told me to pray for her, an ask lined with irony, and I said yes. It was clear she felt like she was too "bad" for God—as if God draws the line at pastor's daughters gargling dicks. I loved that in this woman's eyes, I could just as easily have been going out for the night. Privately, I prayed that she would feel loved as-is.

My story is never going to be the conventional Christian narrative that promises a soapy-clean reputation. And I'm so grateful God made me that way.

**FST!** Susana Perez-Abreu
"Secret Identity" October 2013

When you are born between two countries, your life feels caught between two identities. When I was younger one of my biggest frustrations came from not understanding this beautiful synergy of being a product of the border. As clichéd as it may sound, I ALWAYS felt I was too Mexican for the Americans and too American for the Mexicans.

Every summer my parents would take me to Guaymas, Sonora, to visit my cousins and oftentimes I would feel very awkward because I couldn't relate to their games, they were wearing school uniforms in weird colors like yellow and brown, and they would use words I didn't know. It made me feel I wasn't really Mexican.

But then, I'd come back home and I was one of the ESL kids. When we had to take standardized tests, my name never fit in the bubbles because it was 23 letters long. Even worse, classmates would find out my middle name was "De Jesus" which literally means "of Jesus"; the pride and joy of my Catholic parents. The name situation I won't even get into. Let's just say my older sister knew I was in distress over this and proceeded to fool me well into my adolescence about how my name was "Jessica" in English. Albeit distressing, there was great comfort in my little bicultural, bilingual town; it always appeared everyone around me was in the same boat. There was nothing weird about code-switching, for example. Code-switching is second-nature to us, tu sabes? For the longest time, I had no idea that people didn't naturally habla español and English, así, back and forth, sin pensarla.

Then I went to college and my world changed. I began meeting other people, reading different books, and feeling like I was beginning to own my Chicana identity. I learned about Brown pride and studied thoroughly the writings of Che Guevara. I fell in love with Mexican-American literature, hung a Mexican flag in my dorm room and would walk around code-switching like nobody's business. The Chicano-Hispano Affairs center at the U of A was my safe haven. At that point, I finally felt comfortable embracing the synergy.

Although I was having a great time reclaiming my bicultural identity, there was a great part of me that was innately upset about my situation. When I went to college, I was "allowed" to go under one condition: that I concentrate on school and return home every weekend to keep myself out of trouble. So, being the self-professed good girl I was, I agreed to the terms. My first couple of years I spent every weekend studying and throwing myself into my schoolwork. And every Monday morning, when it came time to return to my little bit of freedom, I was incredibly frustrated that I didn't feel more like an adult. The more I awoke every Saturday morning to my mother's stacks of fresh laundry she had just folded for me, the more I realized I was living a lie.

That's when I developed my secret identity. I thought to myself that if my parents, who I loved, adored, and wanted to make proud wanted me to be a good little Mexican girl, then I would give them that. So, from about age 21-25, I played my good girl role. If staying in Tucson and going to college parties was not an option, then I would have to find ways of having fun and being the "bad girl" I had inside. I found an old high school friend who was still living in Nogales, and together we executed a flawless plan so that I could have fun during my early twenties and not disappoint my parents. I'd arrive Friday afternoons and dedicate time to my parents and siblings. Don't get me wrong, those afternoons are some of the most precious memories I have.

Thoughtful conversations with my dad about politics and Latin American history, girl talk with my mother and sisters, and play time with my nephews. Since my parents were older than your average parents (they had me at 45), it was easy to go out at night without facing the guilt of "leaving them." Every weekend was the same drill. Our family time was over by 9:30 or 10:00 p.m. and I would be free to go. During my nights of debauchery I drank excessively, made-out with strangers, had a mini-fling with a couple of married men, smoked marijuana a few times, and even experienced my first sexual encounter in a car at the age of 21. Although this was not anything developmentally abnormal for someone in his or her early twenties, it was for ME. I can assure you, my mother would have a heart attack if she knew I had been involved in any of these activities.

Each night, as I made my way back home from the Mexican side of the fence, I'd roll all of my windows down, drink lots of water, and sing to the top of my lungs. Arriving home as if I was a good little girl who had gone out to "babysit" her friends was my main objective. And I succeeded. Every Sunday I'd wake up at the ungodly hour of 7 a.m. and go with my parents to Sunday 8 a.m. mass. After mass we'd go to breakfast where they would ask me all about my night. I'd share about how horribly drunk my friends were and what a drag it was to keep them safe. As I think back, I feel a little guilty knowing they were so proud of me. I had managed to gain so much of their trust there was no way they'd ever even entertain the idea that I was going against what our Mexican culture defined as a good, virgin, young lady.

But when I turned 25, something inside me let me know there were one too many things wrong with this picture. For one, the lack of freedom was killing me. At that time, I was a full-grown, college graduated woman whose mother still made her breakfast and washed her clothes. I felt ridiculous. And to add, I slowly began feeling angry at the fact that my parents really didn't love ME, they loved the idea of me... the ideal me. Thirdly, I really resented all of the cultural norms that I was being forced to follow, through no choice of my own. I thought, "If I'm from both worlds, why can't I just choose what works and what doesn't for me?!" And so, in a loud and drastic measure, at 25 years old, I ran away from home. The aftermath was horrible. My parents refused to have a relationship with me; I was practically disowned. To make matters worse, my siblings, who have all followed obediently my parent's requests and desires, reminded me every chance they could how much I had ruined the family's life.

I was incredibly hurt and confused. Mostly because I could not grasp the idea that following my heart and trying to be who I wanted to be was life-ruining to my entire family. I struggled to understand how finding my identity broke theirs. But such is the plight of the Mexican woman. That is our marianismo: a woman, a martyr, a mirror of La Virgen who puts herself before her dreams. I have realized that Mexican women everywhere have a secret identity. Some choose to embrace it, and others, like my mother, deny its existence. But it's there. And its presence is important because it teaches us so many lessons about who we are in the world, about who has the control, about what is wrong with the picture in which we live. In the end, although my guilt sometimes creeps in (and admittedly makes me giggle because I became A MASTER at fooling my parents), had it not been for that secret identity, I would have never found me.

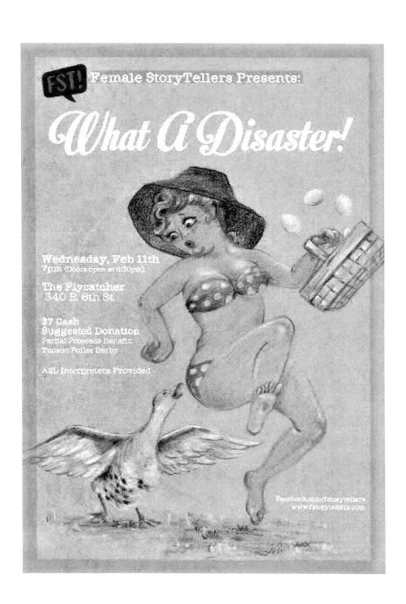

Pink.

In the spring of my 23rd year, I found myself sitting on the one toilet in my three-bedroom basement apartment with plants growing in the wall and snail tracks on the couch.

This was in San Francisco; I was paying $200 to live in a closet that the city was encroaching upon.

I was staring at a stick.

A pink stick.

It had two discernable pink lines on it, even though I had peed on it only 60 seconds ago and was supposed to wait five minutes for my results. Perhaps, I thought, this is one of those things where the lines fade in and out for a while as they are working toward the final tally or whatever.

Like from Barbie to Riot Grrrrl, to salmon flamingo, one line, two lines, ONE! A GAME!

The lines did not fade in and out.

They just got darker and darker and more pink. Riot Grrrrl Barbie with her pet salmon flamingo.

Awesome. I decided I should take a different test to get the results I was looking for. The next test had a plus sign that showed up within two minutes. Pink. I threw up Pepto Bismol.

I called my best friend at the time; we'll call her Mac. I told her I was Pink. "What the fuck does that MEAN?!" she said.

In Golden Gate Park, Mac held my hand and listened to me rage about the damned stripes and plus signs and all the shades of that stupid color and how I had somehow been sucked into a Very Special Episode of Saved by the Bell in which Jessie gets pregnant and has to decide whether she's going to delay becoming president or... dun dun dunnnnnn!!!! Get an abortion! (Gasp!)

I told Mac I was going to get an abortion. She blinked several times.

A little background:

I was a fundamentalist, evangelical Christian until I was 15. Yes, I was embattled in the spirit and Armageddon was nigh. Passionately against abortion right through my sophomore year in high school, I had written and performed a couple of spoken word pieces about it, outlining in detail the lifelong debilitating guilt that would obviously accompany such an act.

By the time Mac and I were having this conversation, I had been steeped in feminism for a few years but had not come around to my own right to choose. Until some short time before I found myself pregnant, I was of the "I would respect someone else's decision to abort, but I would never!" camp. Apparently what I really meant was "I will never find myself unintentionally pregnant and so I don't have to worry about it."

So Mac had a momentary struggle comprehending my desire to terminate. She had been making plans in her head to move in and raise the kid together so I could keep living in the Bay Area and going to college.

She said she wanted to go to the doctor with me. I started crying, "Yes, please."

I made the appointment at what, in my memory, was the only abortion-providing Planned Parenthood in the City at the time, in the Tenderloin, two streets away from where I used to come home to people shooting up in the entryway of my apartment. There was a sad, quiet gathering of eight or ten protesters on the sidewalk in front of the clinic, leaning on those creepy signs of plastic baby parts in Red 40 corn syrup. It was a trip, the Freaky Friday of faith. I thought if I still lived in the small town where I grew up, this would have been a completely different experience. Actually, I probably would already have a couple of kids by this time.

From the entryway to the building where the clinic was, we called up to the office, where they confirmed I had an appointment and was bringing a friend. They buzzed us in through a bulletproof door and directed us to an elevator, which deposited us in front of a bulletproof booth where we were confirmed, again, to have an appointment and buzzed into the office.

In the cozy, pastel waiting room, there were couples and single folks of varying ages sitting around, looking bored, reading magazines or talking about mundane things like who was going to pick the kids up the next day and should we go grocery shopping tonight or tomorrow before work? I sat down with wide eyes. Mac gave my arm a squeeze and asked if I was okay. Frankly, I was a little in shock. I had been expecting an abortion factory full of teenaged women in various stages of pregnancy, draped about the place weeping and shuddering. I did not expect middle-aged women or parents. One very pregnant woman was leaning against her partner, reading a book about birthing, their toddler playing happily with a puzzle at their feet. Some guy came in by himself and got a bag of condoms.

The receptionist gave me a history to fill out and asked if I wanted to see a counselor about my options. I said no counselor, thank you. The person who weighed me and asked all the questions that the nurse would ask again in half an hour wanted to make sure I didn't want to see a counselor before they gave me a cup to pee in to confirm I was pregnant. I was pregnant. The nurse asked if I wanted to see a counselor to talk about it. She was nice and fine with my decision and glad I was fine with my decision, she just wanted to make sure I didn't want to see a counselor. I didn't want to see a counselor. "Okay," she said with this open, understanding look on her face.

"Just let us know if you change your mind."

She sent me into another room to confirm how far along my pregnancy was with an ultrasound.

The picture was this tiny perfect circle within a larger perfect circle. It was breathtaking. I stared at the little print out for so long, in awe of this thing that was in my body, and was my body, and was what my body was doing. I cried. The ultrasound tech, who was disconcertingly very cute, was upset by my tears and threw the photo away quickly, asking if I wanted to see the counselor. I did not want to see the counselor.

I did wish she would have let me keep the ultrasound photo.

Or that I had gotten it out of the trash.

Back in the nurse's office, I had options. I could make an appointment for an in-clinic medical abortion and come back in a week to get it; or, being fewer than eight weeks along, I could get the abortion pill.

The nurse advised the in-clinic abortion. It was usually fast and most people were on their feet and out the door within an hour. The pill seemed less invasive to me at the time. It is possible my years of hearing abortion horror stories from the pulpit may have had something to do with my fear of getting my insides sucked out along with Red 40-covered plastic baby parts. I preferred the privacy of my own home for that kind of experience. The nurse understood.

Only instead of my own home, Mac offered her sunny Berkeley house, which sounded infinitely preferable to the dank, snail-infested hovel where my housemates didn't know I was pregnant, and were certainly not prepared for me to have an abortion in our one tiny bathroom. I was not thinking about Mac's four recently graduated frat brother housemates, and their girlfriends, who had to share the two bathrooms at her house. Logistics are not my strong suit.

I arrived at Mac's at 6 p.m., took the second of two pills, and began a disgusting twelve hour ordeal involving the worst uterine pain I have ever experienced; no fewer than infinity visits to the bathroom; six knocks on the door while I was camped out on the toilet, letting my insides drain out through my vagina; and at least one forgotten toilet flush in the wee hours of the morn. Feel welcome to take a moment to imagine the experience of a hapless young man taking a last pee on his way to bed after a long night of drinking and finding a crimson pool before him. There in the toilet. That he's peeing into.

I could have opted for a simple medical procedure in the clinic that would have taken about an hour and given me several more opportunities to see a counselor. Instead, I went for in-home disembowelment amidst the comforts of a hairy boy bathroom and lots of cheesy romantic comedies featuring apparently straight, probably mostly white, teenagers. I certainly got a story out of it.

The thing that continuously astounded me about all this, and made me want to share my story, is how different my experience was from what I was taught it would be, and not just from my religious background. The stories I'd heard about abortion always involved a very difficult decision made through many tears and sleepless nights, and produced extreme feelings of guilt and regret for the entirety of one's life. Of course that has happened to some. I do not tell this story to take away from their experiences. I tell my story because those are not the only experiences. I was in pain, that's true, but I would have been in pain if I had carried another person in my body for nine months and then given birth. I didn't want that and I never felt guilty about my decision, not once. I never felt like I was making a mistake or giving up an opportunity or betraying my womanhood, or even making a difficult choice.

I felt blessed. I got pregnant and I didn't want to be. I went and got some medicine to make myself not pregnant. It was so simple. In San Francisco, California, where the clinic was a twenty minute bus ride away, with state and private funding that makes abortions available to all women at whatever price they can afford—it was so simple. I had so many resources available to me, the support of my friends, and the complete absence of anyone telling me that this was not my choice to make. It was my choice to make, and I am so thankful that I was enabled to make the right choice for me.

# FST! Sari Beliak
## "Here Comes the Rain Again" August 2016

What is the worst thing you've ever smelled? Okay, I'll go first.

I remember exactly where I was when I smelled the worst smell of my entire life.

January, 2006. St. Bernard Parish, Louisiana.

The stench is burned so deeply into my sinus cavities, that even thinking about that day now triggers a visceral response, bringing me back to that day nearly 10 years ago.

The fridge had been knocked over and it stood at an angle now, supported only by the kitchen cabinets that had broken loose from their molding during the flood. We duct taped the fridge tightly to try to prevent this most horrific assault on our sinuses and everyone stopped what they were doing to help haul it to the curb with the rest of the garbage. But the tile in the kitchen was slick with mud and sewage and the fridge tilted forward on the dolly.

And then, the door burst open.

The smell, a potpourri of rotten fruit, sour milk and spoiled meats that had been submerged and sealed shut in moldy, contaminated flood water for several months, immediately punctured the air like an atomic stink bomb of death before the contents could even spill out, sending hurricane water, broken glass and maggots across the kitchen floor.

The fridge in question had once belonged to a man named Eugene. The knitting room where I was working moments before the fridge burst open had belonged to his wife.

Eugene and his family lived in St. Bernard Parish for years before Hurricane Katrina had destroyed their home, the water rising ten feet in the first fifteen minutes of the storm. When it seemed like Eugene and his family would certainly drown in their own home, a real life miracle arrived: The locked shed in their yard burst open and his small boat broke free and floated towards their window. He loaded his family, including his father who was in a wheelchair, into the small boat and they were able to steer the boat to safety until they could be rescued.

Like most people, I was glued to my TV during Hurricane Katrina and the nightmare of days and weeks that followed in a mix of sadness, frustration, despair and anger. When my brother told me about a volunteer trip to work in New Orleans during his Spring Break with a Jewish student group (he was in college at the time; I was a "Professional Barista" in Los Angeles), I cashed in two free plane tickets and we embarked on one of the most alternative college breaks ever.

We arrived in New Orleans on New Year's Eve. Although the hurricane had hit nearly four months prior, the city was still a clusterfuck of uprooted trees, bent power lines, non-functioning traffic lights, and the National Guard patrolling the streets in Humvees with rifles. Many people had still not returned to their homes since Hurricane Katrina and some probably never would. On the ride from the airport, I stared out the window at the sea of abandoned vehicles that stretched along the underpass for miles. We passed drug stores and Dairy Queens with big, desperate signs that read, "Hiring Immediately, $20/hr," an hourly wage that reflected both the desire to draw people back to rebuild New Orleans and the ghost town that their fantastic city had become.

"All of this was underwater," a local resident told us, gesturing all around where we stood and reaching towards the murky black line approximately ten feet high on the side of his house. Houses had been spray-painted by the National Guard indicating the date they were checked and how many bodies they had retrieved. I thought of a post-apocalyptic story I had read when I was younger, "The Girl Who Owned A City." It was like that, only it was real. And it was devastating.

I stood in what remained of Eugene's home with ten other

volunteers in a mess of mud and mold and overturned furniture and broken glass. His home was completely destroyed.

I had been working in the room adjacent to the kitchen ripping up carpet and bagging up sludgy strings of yarn moments before the smell from the refrigerator (followed by the screams) seemed to pierce through the protective mask I was wearing, sending me and the rest of the volunteers running from the house. We stood in the front yard squealing and retching and laughing, stunned by what had just occurred and that the smell we just encountered was, in fact, a real possible smell that existed.

We had begun working early that morning hauling every item out of the house and dragging it to the curb. Eugene approached me as I was bagging up his wife's porcelain doll collection into garbage bags. He took one from my muddy glove and asked us to save them for her. But after watching us haul out dolls that had become unrecognizable with moldy faces and stringy hair, like we were rescuing them from a swamp, he said "Just forget it. Just throw it away."

I showed him old family photos that seemed like they could have been saved. "Just throw it away," he said, barely looking at the pictures we had lined up along his lawn.

I held them out to him, thinking maybe he didn't realize that I was holding tattered black and white photos of his parents or maybe even his grandparents that could never be replaced.

"Just throw it all away," he said, watching in a daze as strangers quietly and politely carried his possessions to his lawn and placed them in enormous heaps of garbage.

He paused for a moment before he left to go into town. I figured he had changed his mind, maybe the enormity of the scene had taken over and he realized he did want to save some of his pictures.

"If you come across a snow globe with a picture of a boy inside it, please set it aside. It's very important to me."

A snow globe, like the little plastic thing you can buy as a souvenir? I thought to myself. I was sure I had misunderstood, but I agreed and kept working.

"If you didn't find it in the living room, it probably floated away. That's where I used to keep it," he said. "Why is the snow globe so important to you?" I asked, wondering how a snow globe could be more important to this man than old family photos that couldn't be replaced.

"Because it has a picture of my son and his ashes in it."

His words hit me like a punch to the gut. In that moment, I thought of that cliché question, "If there was a fire in your house in the middle of the night and you could only grab one thing, what would you save?" I've probably answered it myself as an ice-breaker at summer camp or as part of some team-building exercise at work, the answers perhaps offering some insight into what I value in my life. Eugene didn't have time to pack a bag of old journals or letters from his grandparents. As his house filled with water and the violent winds ripped off doors and shattered his windows, he only had time to save what was truly important to him—his family.

They lost all of their possessions, but the only thing he wanted was something that represented his baby boy.

I assured him, based on absolutely nothing but my youthful optimism, that we would find his snow globe.

We worked for hours, hauling out furniture and belongings and ripping up moldy carpet from the living room of the house. We sledgehammered out windows and doors. We stripped his house down to the frame. We removed the Fridge of Death.

We removed family photos, couches, wedding albums, porcelain dolls, sports memorabilia, bundles of yarn, clothes, muddy carpet, beautiful crosses, broken dishes, old Playboy magazines and an impressive collection of guns.

There was no electricity in the town where we were, so we worked racing against the sun. We had cleared out every room of the house and still hadn't found Eugene's snow globe. We were tired and hungry and smelled like actual shit.

We were working in the last bedroom in the back of the house. I was shoveling clothes and mud from the closet and passing it to the girl behind me who then loaded the sludge into a wheelbarrow. A mouse darted out of the closet and neither of us even flinched. This shoveling went on uninterrupted like this for a while until she froze for a moment, holding what looked like a wad of mud in her hand.

"Is this... a snow globe?" she asked, trying to wipe the mud off the globe.

She passed it to me and I wiped the sludge on my shirt to reveal a picture of a young boy's face in a snow globe. We cried and cheered and passed the snow globe around the room for all to see, positively elated. We called to the guys working in the room next to us and they ran into the stripped down bedroom and cheered with us.

As the sun was setting, Eugene returned to see the contents of his home in giant heaps on his lawn. He looked around hazily at the piles of furniture and clothes and pictures. We presented him with his son's ashes and he held the snow globe close to his chest.

We loaded into our van, feeling exhausted from the hours of manual labor, yet still high on emotions. We drove away from Eugene's home, now just a bare structural frame stripped down to its exposed bones. He stood on his lawn in stunned silence, surrounded by the piles of his life before Hurricane Katrina, and he held his son's ashes in his hands.

112

"Never Say Never" December 2013

We met on the Ides of March, 1966, in the Cafe Espresso on Tinker Street in Woodstock, N.Y. I was sitting at a table drinking tequila with salt and lime with my friend Cornelia, feeling pretty buzzed when Sheila, the waitress, delivered a drink from Seth. Sheila told me that he couldn't remember my name. I knew him from H. Houst and Son, Woodstock's hardware store where he was the biggest customer who never paid his bills and I was the bookkeeper who never balanced the books. I walked over to the bar to say thanks, already having a bit of a crush on this handsome hulk of a man with the shy smile. I knew his wife, too.

That night after drunken, fumbling, passionate sex he told me that his wife had left him and taken the children to New York City. I didn't know she intended to return home, which she did rather abruptly a few days later and caught us in a delicate position in the downstairs bathroom. She stormed upstairs and Seth drove me home. When he returned he found his suitcase on the front porch, a primitive ritual of divorce amongst the 60's counter-culture.

By now a week had gone by and I was MADLY in love with this man who only had one bag to his name. Before being so abruptly separated from his possessions he had a lovely house on a mountain, a Mercedes, and had just returned from a trip to Europe. In other words, he was a grown up. I was 22, a wildchild exploring the new sexual freedoms the Pill had brought about. He was 32, a mature sophisticated man who drank rum without the coke. Lots of it. And beer. And scotch.

Since he was homeless, he started sleeping in the barn where he stored the equipment and supplies for his house painting business. It was very groovy in the 60's to be working with your hands. Blue collar was the new black. Hey, man, Jesus was a carpenter! Seth just started out by painting his own house and accidentally built up a painting contracting business with six or more employees, a position he was not suited for.

We were in love so it would not do that he was taking up residence in his shop. I was living with my sister in an apartment owned by my father. Daddy had an empty one-room apartment in the same building for $50 a month, so I talked him into renting it to me and my married boyfriend.

We painted the shower stall a teeth-hurting purple and drove to the Sears in Kingston to get a mattress. We put it on the ladder rack of his painting truck and I rode the eleven miles back home on it so it wouldn't blow off. Talk about announcing our new illicit liaison to a small town! A few days later, when I walked into the News Shop to get my morning coffee and hard roll, all eyes turned to me and conversation came to a halt. I got my order to go.

Our apartment was tiny but cozy. A friend gave me a copy of Peg Bracken's "I Hate To Cook" book and I made each recipe in order. I set up my sewing machine and added colorful print pockets to Seth's Brooks Brother's shirts left over from when he had a job in advertising. I even tried ironing, but that was beyond me, so I took his painty work shirts to the cleaners for 25 cents each. I quit my job. I was happily nesting.

All was blissful until he didn't come home from work one night. It got later and later and he still wasn't home. I became frantic with worry. My vivid imagination had him lying in a pool of blood at the bottom of a ladder or pinned under his truck in a gruesome car wreck. But before I called the police, I thought to drive by some of the drinking establishments in town to see if I could find his truck. When I saw it in Deanie's parking lot, I was both relieved and pissed off. Trembling with rage, I marched in and found him at the bar. He turned and I was face to face with his giant sweet grin.

"Oh baby, so good to see you, come and have a drink. Move over and make room for my sweetie." Hmmm, hard to stay angry with such a cheery fellow who put a glass of rum in my hand. The next day, through his hangover, he said he had been feeling a little blue and missed his kids. Poor sensitive and loving guy! Now I really couldn't be angry at him. He swore that it would never happen again. But it did happen again. And again. Each time he would be terribly remorseful for causing me pain and each time I would forgive him thinking that now it would change.

One time on my rounds through town, I couldn't find his truck anywhere. I was in such a panic I even called his wife. She said, "Sometimes he does this—goes out on a binge and doesn't return for a week. You'll be sorry that you took him from me." Five numbing-days later I got a sobbing phone call from Indianapolis, Indiana saying he was so sorry, he hated himself, he was such a horrible person, begging me to I forgive him. And would I send him a plane ticket home. Seems he'd abandoned the truck somewhere and hitchhiked west.

Our reunion was joyful, full of self-recriminations on his part and reassurances on mine. He was so sad I just knew he would change this time. I vowed to love him so much that he would never feel the need to escape again. He thought we should get married and I jumped at the chance. In New York at the time, the only grounds for divorce was adultery and the injured party had to file. His wife wasn't going to so we borrowed $800 from my father so Seth could get a legal Mexican divorce. When he got back we went to the Justice of the Peace to get hitched.

I won't bore you with my codependent doubts and promises to myself that I would leave the next time it happened. We muddled through for about a year, but he could not feel good about himself or his behaviors, so he did the most logical thing he could think of which was to commit himself to Middletown State Mental Hospital. They apparently thought he was nuts too, so they admitted him and put him on Thorazine.

The only thing I learned about Thorazine, besides that it made him drool, is that you can get a wicked sun burn if you spend two hours in the woods on the grounds of the Institution having sex in the sunshine. I thought it was romantic.

After a few months, I got tired of trying to make excuses to his

115

customers with half-painted houses and his employees who needed a paycheck. My friend Cornelia had ventured out West and sent me a postcard saying jobs were plentiful in Denver and apartments were $52.50 a month. It seemed like a good enough place to go, so I told Seth on one of my visits, after having sex in the shade, that I was going to spring him the next week.

I packed the '50 Chevy with everything I thought we would need, including a tablecloth, a dish drainer, some clothes, and my mother's guitar that neither of us could play, and swung by the State Hospital where he was waiting for me out front. Since I'm a crazy optimist, it took me five years and a baby to leave my alcoholic, charming, handsome, crazy, brilliant, self-absorbed, funny, scary, tragic husband. But there, in the parking lot, I jumped out of the car, handed him the keys and went around to the passenger seat. I snuggled up against him as he started the engine and we headed off into the sunset.

# FST! D. Larson
## "The Long Way 'Round" June 2015

It took me a decade to graduate from college.
I signed up for Pima Community College in August 1998, about a week shy of my 18th birthday. My parents drove me the hour and a half to Tucson from Sierra Vista to register me for classes.

"You can move to Tucson," my dad said. "But only if you go to college."

Since I hadn't passed the math and science classes necessary to apply for the U of A, Pima was my second best bet. I didn't want to go to college, but I would have done anything to move out of my parents' house. My relationship with my dad was rocky, at best.

In addition, I was failing at recovering from an eating disorder (recovering is what I pretended I was doing, both to others and to myself), and I had zero interest in school or a career. A good friend had invited me to live with her in Tucson, so I thought I'd do that.

"Get a marketable skill," my dad told me, over and over again. "Like an X-Ray tech. Or a lawyer. You like to argue with me. You should become a lawyer."

My first year in Tucson was an adjustment. I was incredibly homesick. Instead of studying, I spent all my time smoking pot with my best friend, who was a senior in high school and drove to Tucson on the weekends. We'd get high and ride the streetcar, buy carrot cake from Coffee Plantation, or go to the movies, paid for with my credit card. I spent the other part of the time going to work at a bagel shop, drinking beer after beer until I cried, reading everything but my homework, and writing sad poetry in my journal. I avoided cleaning the house, much to the annoyance of my roommates.

I learned how to ride the bus. I could read the bus schedule, obtain a transfer, and somewhat successfully avoid the endless stream of men who sexually harassed me. I wore headphones, a large jacket even on sunny days, and gave fake names, fake numbers, and a fake age...16.

I was Sally, the 16-year old with a boyfriend, who was definitely not interested, not even in the guy who rubbed his crotch on me as we stood in the aisle of a crowded bus. When we got off the bus, he asked me for my number. I wish I'd told him to fuck off, but I'm pretty sure I told him I had a boyfriend.

In my second year in Tucson, I decided to become a radical feminist. My eating disorder had pretty much subsided, and I'd stopped smoking pot and binge drinking, which led to much happier and more positive day-to-day thoughts and feelings.

I worked in the periodicals section of library and spent the majority of my time reading back issues of Ms. Magazine and becoming politically aware. I spent the other part of my time updating my radical feminist blog, which was filled with all the "fuck yous" I wish I'd said to the men on the bus (now I had a car).

I joined a feminist activist group, Las Sinfronteras. I became a radical cheerleader, which combined my love for performance with my newfound love of feminist politics. We wore red and black cheerleading skirts, black tank tops, and crudely formed the words "RAD CHEER" out of red duct tape and pasted them on our clothes. We performed all over Tucson, sneering at our audiences, flipping them off, and chanting "Racist, sexist, anti-gay! You can't take our streets away!"

We opened for Le Tigre, combining music, performance art, and radical cheerleading. I met my idol, Kathleen Hanna, who put her arm around me for a photo, talked to me like an equal (I was 20 years old and STARSTRUCK), and told me to send my photos of the event to her. I admired her exceptionally hairy armpits and mumbled a few words about how much I loved her and how inspirational she was to me.

Needless to say, I didn't get much homework done, but I wasn't very interested, anyway.

My third year in Tucson, I transferred to the U of A, declared an English major, did a year, flunked out, and was kicked out of college. I was so depressed about my inability to do school (despite the fact that I didn't really want to put in any effort), that I decided to get a therapist, who reminded me, gently, that perhaps school just wasn't my thing right now.

So I went to work at a record store for minimum wage, did half a year of working full time, realized how much school WAS my thing (or at least learning was), and promptly signed up for a Study Skills class at Pima, which I paid for with my hard-earned money.

My fourth, fifth, sixth, and part of my seventh year in Tucson were spent working at that record store, taking Journalism classes, and slowly earning my Associate's degree. I hadn't bothered to earn it before transferring to the U of A.

At the record store, I learned how to successfully handle drug addicts selling stolen CDs, the smelly guy who licked the wrinkles out of his money before handing it over, teenage shoplifters (they always cried), and Juggalos, who kept our store in business by buying far more Insane Clown Posse CDs and merchandise than they stole. I learned about 70s punk, post-punk, pop-punk, emo, screamo, modern jazz, shoegaze, indie rock, glam rock, classic country, and more about various subgenres of metal and rap than I ever cared to.

On weekend nights we hired policemen to help us keep the peace. Most signed up for the gig because they loved music and wanted to get paid to shop. One Friday night I asked a customer to leave his duffel bag at the front of the store, next to the cop who was on the job that night. He did, reluctantly but not rudely. He found a CD, paid for it, grabbed his duffel bag, swung it over his shoulder, and set off the alarm. The policeman asked to see the contents of his bag. Inside was a sawed-off shotgun, several rounds of ammunition, several cans of spray paint and a pound of meth. The metal content in his bag had likely set the alarm off. The policeman called for backup and told our customer sternly that he would be going away for a very, very long time.

He turned, gave me a devastated look, his eyes beginning to water, and said, "All I wanted was a CD."

At the end of my seventh year in Tucson, I graduated from Pima with my AA degree in Liberal Arts.

My eighth year in Tucson I returned to the U of A to start a Journalism program. I had to jump through a million hoops to be readmitted. I submitted form after form, stating why I had failed at college the first time, and how I thought I could do better this time, as evidenced by my good grades at Pima, my willingness to attend therapy, and my Study Skills class, which had turned me into a master of homework and organization.

The Dean of Social and Behavioral Sciences laughed at me when I asked him what other signatures I had to get. He smiled and told me his was the last one, and I was now officially a student at the University of Arizona.

My ninth year in Tucson the recession hit and I was let go from the record store. I had worked there for five years. I churned out story after story in Journalism school, all on deadline. I still didn't like school, although I was now able to make certain compromises to be able to get my degree, like suck it up and do my homework, go to bed at a reasonable hour, and turn down invitations from friends when I had a paper due.

My tenth year in Tucson I took my last two classes in summer school and FINALLY graduated from the University of Arizona with a B.A. in Journalism and a minor in Women's Studies in August of 2008.

I wish I could say my graduation was a monumental occasion, but it felt largely anticlimactic. I heard my name called, had my picture taken, and walked up to the podium to receive my diploma. That was it, and ten years of wondering if I'd ever get my degree was over.

Sometimes I wish I'd made choices for myself that would have allowed me to graduate in four or five years. My life likely would have been easier, or at least I imagine that it would have been so, but it would have lacked the color of these experiences, and I doubt I would have learned so much along the way.

 Erin Jaye
## "I Can't Believe That Just Happened" January 2013

So these jeans are a little snug. Too many carbs over the holidays. Too many delicious, comforting, glorious carbs. I may never love another human being the way I love me some chocolate cake.

Have you ever had the Sour Cream Chocolate Cake at Blue Willow? So good! Ladies, next time you have PMS, get yourself a slice or two.

If you've ever had brunch at Blue Willow on a Sunday, you know there's always a wait. People love some mimosas and overpriced buckwheat pancakes, lemme tell ya. Luckily, when I was working there in college, I was a pretty shitty waitress, so they never made me work that crazy shift. Too busy, couldn't handle it. So, I worked Sunday nights, instead. Slow, steady, safe Sunday nights for Erin. But every now and then I'd cover a shift for someone and work a double. Help someone out, make some extra money.

Well, during one of these Sunday a.m. shifts I'd picked up, I looked out onto the patio to see if I'd had any new tables. I notice this woman by the bussers' station, her back turned to me, bent over the garbage can, and she was... kind of moving funny, and I'm thinking, "Is that lady throwing up? Jesus, you'd have to knock back a lot of mimosas to be ralphing half way through brunch." But I guess better in the bin than on the table, right?

I quickly realize, though, that no, she's not throwing up, and that her funny movement was because she's hitting something. She's hitting a baby. On its back. Over a garbage can, in a restaurant. Oh my God. It's choking, the baby's choking. And she's still hitting it, so it's still choking. So, whatever she's doing isn't working. And that's at least 30 seconds now that that baby hasn't been breathing, plus however long this was happening before I noticed, that that baby's brain isn't getting oxygen. Every second I stand here, every second this restaurant full of people stay sitting at their tables, every second this continues to go on are accumulating seconds increasing the baby's chances of suffering brain damage or dying.

And fuck that noise!

I turn around, run to the hostess station, bark at the hostess "There's a baby choking, call 911, now," turn back around, run up to the lady, reach for the baby, and she just dumps him into my hands, apparently trusting that this 20-year-old waitress has a plan or is a medical student or something. The latter was certainly not the case. I did have to learn adult and infant CPR in high school, though. Anyone else? Awkwardly practicing on a vaguely male mannequin while some douche bag on the lacrosse team encourages you to use tongue? Good times.

So yes, I was CPR-certified and had learned the Heimlich maneuver. That was only a few years before this incident with the baby, so I still remembered what I'd learned. Well, I was about to find out if I did, anyway.

So, I've got the baby boy, he's around 18 months, curly, dark blond hair. And I'll never forget the look of panic and confusion on his tiny face. Even if he could breathe, he was too young to speak, but his face was saying, "Why can't I breathe? What's going on?"

I rush him into the gift shop, by the hostess station, where the hostess is on the phone with the emergency operator. The woman from whom I'd snatched this baby, and a younger woman who turned out to be the mother, followed. The hostess and the women are talking, frantically answering the 911 operator's questions about the baby's age, health, etc., and I sit on the floor by the door to try and get some fucking oxygen to this kid's brain.

He was still conscious. First, I tried hitting him on the back again, followed by a finger sweep, first with my pinky, then with my index finger because I wasn't feeling anything. But even with my adult index finger going all the way down his infant esophagus, still, nothing.

At this point he loses consciousness. I decided to try the Heimlich. I

123

lay him down on his back, measured two fingers below his tiny sternum, placed my left index and middle fingers on top of my right index and middle fingers, and gently but firmly thrust down and upwards a few times, then swept my finger across his mouth, scooping into his little throat for the evil little piece of cantaloupe that the women said he'd been eating.

Nothing. Jesus, fucking, Christ, why is he still not breathing? There is nothing in his throat. I can't believe this is happening. I can't believe this isn't working. I can't believe this kid is going to die, in my fucking arms. I don't want to believe that, I'm not going to believe that until he is, in fact, dead.

(The fact that I had promised his hysterical mother, who was also on the floor, that I would not let her son die [who the fuck says that?! Don't say that!], that everything was going to be fine, that the ambulance would be there any second, made the pressure about 10,000% worse.)

Ok, panic and desperation are setting in. I know that mouth-to-mouth isn't going to do a damn thing if his airway is blocked, but at this point, what the fuck else am I going to do, twiddle my thumbs and stare at the dead baby lying in my lap? Thank you, no. So, I go for it.

I tilt his chubby little face, which is now blue, back. I never knew a person could actually be the color blue (I'll thank the Arrested Development fans in the house for forgiving my avoidance of a Tobias joke during this particular story). I plug his nose, wipe some of the drool from around his mouth with my sleeve—not for sanitary reasons, but because it would prevent me from making a seal around his lips—and I blow gently.

Nothing's going in. I worry I'm hurting him. I mean I know he can't feel anything because he's unconscious, but he's just so little and I'm so big and felt brutish handling his little body like that.

At some point the phone was passed to me and the operator asked if he had a pulse. I checked his wrist, then his neck, but I couldn't feel a thing, except his silky-smooth baby skin, which was bluer still.

So here I am, sitting on the floor, surrounded by customers and coworkers, with a blue, dead, baby in my arms.

The mother who I had, it would now seem, lied to about saving her baby, may or may not have still been screaming because I don't remember what was happening around me at that point.

I hear the sirens and think, "Oh my God, if they'd gotten here just a little bit sooner."

Right after I first heard the sirens, I heard something else. A faint gurgle. Which turned into long, slow, labored gasps. It was simultaneously the most awful thing I'd ever heard—a baby desperately trying to breathe—and the best, most miraculous sound I'd ever heard.

"I can't believe it. How is this happening?" I thought. I'd stopped trying because it wasn't working and I could hear the sirens, so how did he just suddenly start breathing?

Well, by the time the medics came inside and put the oxygen mask on him, he'd progressed from tight gasps to full breaths, on his own, from blue-faced and silent to red-faced and wailing.

Now I'm standing, being ushered towards an ambulance by an EMT carrying the oxygen tank that was attached to the mask now on baby's face. I was explaining to him that the baby just suddenly started breathing, that nothing I'd done had worked. He was telling me I was brave and did everything right and that my son would be fine.

"Wait, no. No, he's not my son. I just work here." I looked all around. "Where's his mom? His mom should be with him."

When the EMT realized I was just some chick, no relation to the baby, he gently took him and got into the ambulance.

I felt horrible letting go of that baby. I wanted to stay with him and be sure he was okay and not afraid.

As the ambulance pulled out, I walked back inside and finally saw how many people had been around me and had seen what had happened, how shocked they all looked.

A couple of the women I worked with were crying, and when my manager, Stephanie, hugged me and said she was proud of me, the intensity and fear and desperation and everything I hadn't felt because of the adrenaline, hit me like a ton of bricks and I, too, burst into sobs.

"Go home. Just, go home. It's okay," my manager said.

There was so much about that event that I couldn't believe.

Initially, I couldn't believe that no one else was doing anything. I wasn't the first person to notice this; I wasn't even on the patio. I mean, a restaurant full of people, other parents, mothers. "What about maternal instinct?" I wondered.

During it, I couldn't believe that what I was doing wasn't working. At all. "Am I doing it wrong? I swear that's how they taught us. Why won't he breathe?"

Well, it turns out there wasn't any damn cantaloupe in his throat. There wasn't anything in his throat. He had some condition that apparently caused his trachea to suddenly close up. Neither the mother, nor the woman with her, mentioned this when the 911 operator asked about his health, etc.

So, nothing I could have done (short of a tracheotomy, maybe) could have helped him. His fit passed just in time. A coincidence, or a miracle, or whatever. I could not believe that either.

Afterward, I couldn't believe I'd reacted the way I did. Grabbing someone's child from them, yelling at customers to back off and shut up so I could hear what my coworker was relaying from the 911 operator, pumping an infant's chest. A complete lack of inhibition. Perhaps bordering on irresponsible? Did I really know what the hell I was doing? What if I'd broken his little ribs? What if… I'd gotten sued?

What I could least believe—less than the fact that it happened, that I went all Doogie Howser MacGyver on the situation, that he wasn't even choking, that what I did had no effect on his having lived or died—was that he didn't die.

I mean, he was dead. He was blue. I couldn't feel a pulse. He hadn't been breathing for several minutes (though it felt like ages). He was effectively dead. But he woke up, and he started breathing, on his own.

I saw his mom and him at the grocery store the next year. She didn't recognize me. But I didn't care. I wanted to say something, but being the queen of awkward that I am, I just hung back and watched him for a minute, so grateful for his chubby face, that it was not blue at all.

My family, friends, and students know I can be intense and inflexible about certain things. It's a part of my nature. On a daily work/relationship/life basis, I genuinely strive to pause and think before I act, so as to not react. And I think that overall, I do a pretty decent job.

But either way, at the end of the day, at the end of this story, I wouldn't change this aspect of my personality.

I'm at peace with who I am, truly. Because I'd rather be the person who overreacts to a false alarm, than be one of a room—or restaurant—full of people that would watch the real deal go down, and do nothing, only to say afterwards, feeling wretched, "I can't believe that just happened."

Now, who wants to take a CPR class with me? That shit's changed since I was in high school 12 years ago!

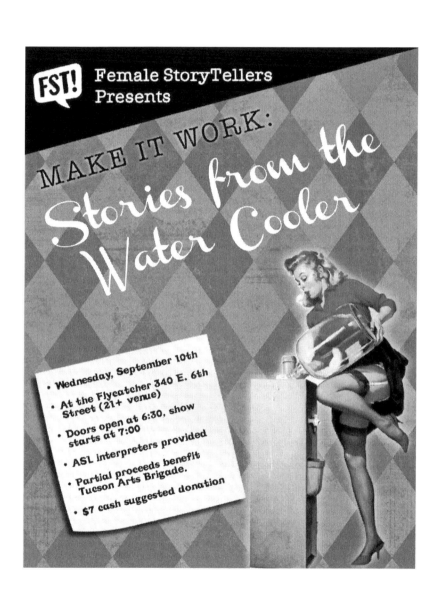

FST! Annie Conway
## "Make it Work" September 2014

My first "real," i.e. non-babysitting, job was working in the kennel of a vet's office for a couple of hours a day after school. I was 16. I was not then, nor am I now, a huge animal lover. I have never had a desire to be a vet, or a marine biologist, or lion tamer, and, despite the current animal count at my house, am really meh about most animals. But the idea of working and having that real job—where I made $5.50 an hour—was so appealing. The job only lasted a few months because then my high school got toxic mold and shut down and I had to go to school in the afternoons. That's a story for another time. But I had a taste for working and I liked the sense of accomplishment and independence it brought. And having my own money was really exciting!

Fast forward nearly ten years and I had my first "real" job post college: working in social services. Using my degree and making double my first job's hourly pay. Yep, I was in the double digits! Hello, $11! I felt like a real adult and contributing member of society. I had benefits and everything! Going to the doctor and handing over a card with my name on it, not my parents', was remarkably satisfying. Paying the stupidly large copay was less so.

Things were good. The job was exhausting, emotionally draining, and really hard. Honestly, I had no idea what I was doing for the first year or so. But I had some absolutely amazing mentors who encouraged me and helped me learn. After three years, I felt really good at my job. And I'd gotten a raise! Hey there $12.33—you're looking mighty fine!

Then they announced there would be layoffs and everyone had to reapply and re-interview for their job. I figured, I got this, I'm good at my job, and my supervisors like me. At this point, I have three years of experience. They hired me with next to none, so this should be a breeze. I did my résumé and cover letter and went to the interview with everyone else. We sat in the waiting room while they called each

129

of us back for about 20 minutes. I waited, I walked back when called, I smiled, I answered the questions—quite well I might add—and I felt good. This was probably the best interview I'd ever had. After all, what makes a person better qualified for a job than currently doing the EXACT job?

In hindsight, I can see how ridiculous and manipulative this was. You made me reapply and interview for a job I already had? This wasn't a promotion; this wasn't an annual review. It was a complete application and interview. When they asked why I was qualified, I basically said "Cuz I've worked here for three years and I already have the job." But in a nice way.

The day came when we were told if we had a job or not. A few of my coworkers readily admitted they were gonna be cut. They knew they were slacking or loud mouths, but no one thought it would be me. I was called back down a hallway in the administration building and told I wasn't a good fit for the team. So I asked why. They said I didn't have the right experience. I was stunned. I had nothing to say, so I walked out of the room. Mind you, I had trained every person they kept with the "right experience."

As I walked out to my waiting friends, I just shook my head and started to cry because I really loved my job. They gasped in disbelief, rushed to hug me, said "It'll be ok," and we all said a collective "Fuck you, we're better off!"

The first week of my unemployment, there was a lot of drinking. And it was fun. All my friends got laid off too, so there was no shortage of drinking buddies and bitching time. The second week, I got serious and applied for a few more jobs. I went online and hit all the job sites: Monster, Jobing, etc. and I had a resume and cover letter all ready to go, so that was convenient. It was now 2005 and we had hit full-on recession. There weren't tons of openings, but I wasn't worried. There were enough and I knew I'd get something. Three years ago, I got a job in three weeks with nearly no experience. This would be a breeze. I was such a good candidate and I had so much experience and great references. Not worried at all. Third week came, no job yet. Fourth week, no job and no calls. That's when things started to suck.

I couldn't travel because I had no money and I had to be in town. What if someone called me for an interview? So I was home all day, alone. I watched a lot of cooking shows. I can now chop an onion like nobody's business. And I decided I want to grow up and be Ina Garten. All my friends were finding jobs or going to school and suddenly I was the only one looking.

I felt lost. And I felt guilty for feeling lost. I was 25. Single, no kids, no debt, great family. My parents had let me know if I needed help with rent or anything, they were there for me. I didn't need money. I lived pretty cheaply and I just stopped doing anything. I got unemployment, which was about $900 a month. Know what that gets you? Rent, utilities, food, and, dammit, I kept cable because what the hell else was I gonna do all day? But I was still so lost.

I hadn't realized how much my job had defined me. I was proud of it and proud of myself. I knew I was good at something. I liked it and I felt confident. I knew I could handle any crazy situation that arose because I had handled so many crazy situations. More than once, I stumbled through my poor Spanish to get information and reassure a new client who was scared and alone. I answered the crisis line and heard horrific stories. I can talk about the dynamics of power and control and its complexities and subtleties for hours. But every time I thought about my job, I was in disbelief and I was angry. I cried. A lot. I felt sorry for myself and had some damn good pity parties.

But then my brother called. He and I have had our ups and downs, but somehow he got it. He'd recently been out of a job for a while. And he got it. The frustration. The self-doubt. The loss of self. I didn't know who I was. And he gave me good advice. Well, sort of. "Get out and play basketball." Seriously, basketball? Have we met? But I got his point. Go outside. Go for a walk. See a movie. Just get out. He convinced me to drive to Phoenix at one point for a concert. He asked me if I wanted to go. I asked if he had friends that wanted to go. He asked me again. I said the gas prices were kind of high. He said he'd pay for my gas (I'm confident he didn't, but that wasn't actually a legit excuse). He asked again and I finally agreed. And that's how I ended up seeing Bone Thugs-N-Harmony live. I felt like a little bit of a badass.

I was unemployed for 3 months. I got a job doing more or less the same work, but getting paid more. Ha, take that! I didn't do anything drastic. I didn't need money from my parents. I survived on unemployment. I was just fine. But I was shaken and I swore I wouldn't let that happen again. I wouldn't "be" my job. I wouldn't define myself by my work. I wouldn't fall in love. And, for the next three years, I didn't.

Before I really realized it, I had fallen in love again. With another new job. I chose to spend my days surrounded by silly, dramatic tweens, and I loved it. Every moment of it—good and bad. And then the news came. Layoffs. Again. But this time, I had some warning and things didn't feel vindictive or underhanded. When the final word came that I was laid off, for the second time in my 20's, I had a better handle on things. There were still lots of tears and lots of drinking, but I knew I'd be ok. Luckily, I only had to go a couple of months before HR called and offered me another job. I think I said "YES!" before they even said what the job was. Because the reality was, it didn't matter. I still needed a job. I'm lucky because it's been great, overall. As devastating as losing a second job that I loved was, I decided it's okay to love my work. It makes me better at what I do. And frankly, it's worth it.

## "Under the Influence" October 2014

There was and there was not milk, breast milk that is. But first there was a baby, a Juniper Ruth to be exact. And before all of this, there was an uncertain mother—me. The desire to have children was slow to evolve in me, and I had hoped in a way that it would pass, but it didn't. Every step of the way I felt uncertain about mothering, but the one thing I never felt uncertain about was breast milk.

I was clear about the amazing awesomeness of breastfeeding; that milk from my body could nourish another living being I found to be nothing short of miraculous. And so, prior to the arrival of Juniper Ruth, I read and learned everything I could about breastfeeding. I attended La Leche League meetings and joined other pro-breastfeeding groups in Tucson. I created a robust community of mothers and soon-to-be mothers bound together by a commitment to breastfeeding.

Juniper Ruth arrived after a long three-day labor. I was exhausted but I was also elated. She was beautiful and so awake and, most importantly to me, she was a perfect breastfeeder. No latch problems, no tongue-tie, no jaundice. In my mind, I had just gotten a gold-star in mothering because, even after an induction, we were rock stars in the breastfeeding department.

By the end of her first week, though, we were no longer rock stars. She was screaming her head off during and after every nursing. She would latch and unlatch, always seemed hungry, and would only sleep in half hour stretches. My husband reassured me that babies are fussy—it would pass. I tried to use my breast pump one night, when nursing was just not working at all, and got no milk. I started to worry.

But all my reading and the pro-breastfeeding community I had built reassured me and encouraged me not to give in, or up. The common, repeated rhetoric: "You will at some point think you don't have enough milk, don't succumb to this fear, don't supplement with formula. Work hard at breastfeeding, it is just hard." And so I reflected on all of this and convinced myself that my fears were misguided. "Perhaps she is just really colicky," my husband added.

At our two-week pediatric visit, though, numbers confirmed my nagging fears. She had stopped gaining weight and, in fact, was significantly below her birth weight. The pediatrician asked me to nurse more often and come in for weight checks every other day. After the third weight check he finally said, "You need to supplement."

Now, maybe to other mothers this wouldn't have been a big deal, but in my brain, breastfeeding exclusively and being a good mom were one and the same. I felt like I had failed. I cried the whole way home. And then, at some point between the pediatrician's office and my house, all logical thought left my brain: I decided that the pediatrician was wrong and that I was still going to exclusively breastfeed. And so began my crazy breastfeeding month—where for four weeks my entire life was breastfeeding.

I put myself on a nursing schedule where I tried to nurse and pump every hour around the clock, which meant perhaps ten minutes of every hour was not dedicated to extracting milk from my boobs. I took herbs, changed my diet, hired lactation consultants, rented a hospital-grade pump, drank barley water, and tried a prescription drug that is difficult to get and expensive. But as we approached Juniper's six-week birthday, it became clear that these efforts were not working. I was going insane due to sleep deprivation (and not in a funny sort of way). My husband was beyond worried. My pediatrician was getting hysterical. Juniper Ruth still seemed hungry and had only gained a little weight.

And so with many tears and pounds of maternal guilt, I finally bought some formula and gave it to her. Shockingly to me, the world didn't end; the breastfeeding gods didn't strike me down with a bolt of lightning. Juniper Ruth slept for three hours straight for the first time in her life. I didn't have the world's most colicky baby; just a hungry one. I felt horrible. I had failed at breastfeeding and had starved Juniper for a good six weeks.

Intertwined with this overwhelming guilt, though, was a rising sense of anger. Because in truth, my educational background and the pro-breastfeeding community that I had surrounded myself with had completely intoxicated me. I like to use the analogy of beer goggles—how drinking a lot of alcohol makes you see everyone as being really attractive. Well, I had put on breastfeeding goggles; it was like I just couldn't see the reality of how hungry Juniper was and how much my dedication to breastfeeding was ruining our lives. And, even worse, when I gave her that first formula and finally started to see more clearly, my beautiful, pro-breastfeeding community tore me to shreds.

I was out for one of the first times with Juniper Ruth and was giving her a bottle after I had already breastfed her and a woman came up to me and said, "You are being so selfish not breastfeeding and feeding your daughter that poison instead." In the mom/baby groups I attended, I got chastised for not trying hard enough to make breastfeeding work. I was told I was ruining her health, that she would have allergies and diabetes. I was told to pump more, work harder, and find another pediatrician. I was so hurt, and then I was enraged.

Because, at the end of the day, once I began to see my reality clearly, the choice in front of me was to feed my hungry baby or cling to my ideal of exclusively breastfeeding. That is not a choice; hungry baby always wins. It pissed me off that my community couldn't and wouldn't support this clarity.

At the two-month mark, I was giving Juniper formula and breast milk, but I still had an addict-like attachment to breastfeeding. I was hoping that eventually all of the herbs, diet changes, and the prescription drug I was taking would work and I would be able to wean her off formula. Thankfully, though, I saw a nurse on Christmas Eve who finally cured me of my addiction.

She listened empathetically to my story and she said the exact thing I needed to hear: "Breast milk is amazing but so is joy. You have worked really hard and Juniper is getting breast milk, but what you and your family need is joy." And that was it. I sobered up. I stopped being so dedicated and started enjoying my daughter.

And so, if I were ever to run into that woman who criticized me in public for bottle-feeding, I would, of course, say "Fuck You." But the truth is, she was right. I was being selfish, selfish in my attachment to breastfeeding. And I was feeding my baby poison, the poison of non-stop stress and anxiety over breastfeeding.

Juniper Ruth and I breastfed and bottle-fed for two years. She is healthy and happy by all accounts. And, although I may not be confident in a lot of the choices I make as a mother, I am confident that I made the right choice about milk—that choosing joy over breast milk was the right choice. My only regret now is that I didn't choose joy sooner.

When I was four, my birth mother died, leaving me and my three older sisters—Amy, age 17, Patty age 15 and Sandi age 14—in the care of her sister, our Aunt Ginny... who had four teenagers of her own plus three more part time children from her second marriage. That's a lot of numbers.

Amy took this transition as an opportunity to drop out of school, get a tattoo and marry her then-boyfriend. Patty took it as an opportunity to drop out of school, run away and do a shit-ton of drugs. Sandi and I stayed with Ginny for a while. With at least ten years separating me and the eight other children in the house, a decision was made. Sandi begged Ginny not to, promised to drop out of school and care for me full time, but the decision to put me up for adoption was a done deal.

Ginny still calls it her Sophie's Choice, which pisses my (adoptive) mom off. Far from the Nazis at Auschwitz, I was adopted by a liberal, middle class, Stanford-educated couple with season tickets to the symphony and two young boys. The transition from one upper middle class Stanford educated liberal family to another was traumatic, as you can imagine, so to ease this difficult time for me, Sandi would stay with me as much as possible. We started with weekends at the new family's house, then gradually weekends at Ginny's. And when I moved in with my new family, Sandi still visited often. She taught me how to braid my hair and all the words to Paperback Writer by The Beatles.

For the next three years, many of my weekends were spent with Sandi, hearing about how much trouble the world was in, about the need for radical peace, and how, when I got older, I'd learn how a weekend in the redwoods on peyote would open my mind and soul.

Sandi hand-made a lot of the clothes I wore and every piece she made came with a little tag that said "Especially hand made by Sandi." When she'd make herself something, she'd use the leftover scraps to make hair bows for me, the only ones I'd use at the ends of my long braids.

So certain was I that Sandi knew best, I couldn't understand why everyone was so upset when she followed in her sisters' footsteps and dropped out of school just two months before graduation. The way she explained it to me—that the diploma was just a piece of paper and that true learning would only happen by experiencing life, not sitting in a classroom with a bunch of brainless puppets—made perfect sense to me.

From then on, for the next seven years or so, I anxiously awaited the letters she'd send, written in her casually perfect handwriting. In 1982, she joined the Guardian Angels—they were like a neighborhood watch group on steroids—and Sandi sent me a picture of her and her new friends in their matching red berets on the mean streets of Portland.

My sister was a crime-stopping superhero!

In 1984, a letter informed me that she was basically married to the hairy guy in the picture next to her, the one in the suede boots. They weren't going to get legally married since that was just an institution of The Man. But they were having a beautiful time following the Dead and living communally out of the van in the background of the picture. The letter also said that, even though she was smoking in the picture, it wasn't okay for me to.

My sister was such a free spirit!

In 1986, there was no picture, but she wrote that she was now a Hell's Angel and married to a guy named Skip with the most bitchin' Harley she'd ever seen. She didn't wear a white dress to the wedding, instead she wore jeans and these black cowboy boots with red flames that Skip had bought her.

My sister was so cool.

Sometimes, I'd get a phone call. I'd tell her about my life in Suburbia. She'd ask if I was still taking piano lessons, which I was. She'd ask if I'd kissed a boy yet, which I had. She asked if I'd had sex yet, which EW, I hadn't. I'd tell her about the school play and this really funny guy on TV named David Letterman.

She'd tell me she loved the sound of my voice and I could hear her smiling through the phone. I'd ask her when she was coming to visit and she'd change the subject and tell me she loved me and call me her baby.

And I wished I was brave and strong and free like my sister.

But when I was 14 or so, it all stopped—no more letters, no more phone calls, no explanation.

Over the next 16 years, as you can imagine, I often wondered about her—where she was, what she was doing, who she was with. Maybe she was in jail. Some days I was convinced she was dead. Drug overdose, maybe.

In my weaker moments, I tried to imagine what I'd done to chase her away. Every couple years my mom would ask tentatively, "Do you ever hear from Sandi?" I'd shake my head and say "I just wish I knew if she was alive."

And really, that's all I wanted. Proof—one way or the other.

Then one afternoon, 16 years after I'd spoken to her last, the phone rang. I was home with my 3-month old baby boy who had just fallen asleep in my lap. I rushed as gently as I could to pick up the phone hoping not to wake him.

"Hello?"

"Is this Maryann?" the voice on the other end asked.

"Who's this?" I asked, already knowing, already shaking.

139

Sandi asked how I was doing as casually as you can imagine. "Good. I'm good. ???"

She asked what I was up to. "I just got home from work and I'm holding my baby boy." She wanted to know what he looked like. "He looks just like my husband. He's blonde and has blue eyes. I don't know where those came from because mine are brown."

"Mine are blue," she said. "So were Mom's."

Over the next three years, I heard from her almost every day. Some days I'd get five or six emails from her in one day. Her husband was on his third tour in Iraq and she was lonely. She'd tell me how her ignorant neighbors drove her crazy or about an article she'd read in the paper. She'd write out the dream she'd had the night before in intricate detail, or relay the destructive antics of one of her five pets. She'd tell me how she refuses to pay some asshole to overcharge her to get the TV fixed, so she'll just live without 'til Ben comes home.

But there were fourteen years that she never told me a single story about. As far as I could tell, her life ended fourteen years ago, the last time we spoke on the phone, and started again when she met Ben and he helped her "clean her life up."

Sometimes I'd ask and she'd say something like "I didn't do much I'm proud of." See, part of her was always afraid I wouldn't like her anymore if I knew. And part of me was always afraid she'd disappear again if I asked, so I didn't push it. But now I know I'll never have to worry about her disappearing ever again, no matter what.

See, about three years after that afternoon phone call, Sandi was diagnosed with Stage 4 lung cancer. The doctors told her she had weeks, maybe months to live. So I bought a plane ticket to Georgia and, for the first time in nearly twenty years, I saw my sister Sandi.

She was in the hospital, covered in tubes. She was fat and had grey hair and grey skin. When she tried to smile, I could see that her teeth were crooked, and some were sort of brown. I was almost afraid of her for a second, the way little kids are sometimes afraid of the elderly or people in wheelchairs.

Then she opened her mouth to speak—she couldn't make noise but she moved her lips. I came to her side and we began to talk. I held her hand and brushed back her hair. I adjusted her pillows and blankets when she asked and called for the nurse when she needed one.

Her doctors told me I was the only one who could read her lips. "Of course I can. She's my sister."

I told her how I'd been swimming just a couple days earlier and as my air bubbles passed my goggles with each breath, I'd wished I could breathe for her. She mouthed "You make me stronger. You make be braver. You make me better."

My visit was short, just two days, and she died before I could see her again. I was left with a feeling that she'd abandoned me again.

But a couple of weeks after she died, her husband sent me a box. In it was a pair of grey fuzzy clogs, a pair of flowered Doc Martens and a pair of black cowboy boots with red flames which, Ben explained, he'd never seen her wear, but that she polished once a month like clockwork since he'd known her. And wouldn't you know it, we wore the exact same size shoe. They fit like a glove.

Shortly after that, I had a dream that I'd moved into a house with her in Portland, Oregon (where we were born) to care for her in her final days. Just before I woke up, she told me I'd done all I could for her and that it was time for me to go home. So no, she hadn't abandoned me.

Also in that box from her husband were some clothes she thought I might like to have in the dressing room, in the theatre where I work. Among these items was a gorgeous brown suede jacket with fringe down the arms. It sat in the closet, still wrapped in dry-cleaning plastic for a couple years before anyone wore it. Trevor, one of my Advanced Drama students, was the first to try it on and when he put his hand in the pocket he found a note, written in my sister's casually perfect handwriting. "Put it down, Trevor." the note said. So no, she's not gone.

In fact, now my students love telling freshmen the story of how the theatre is haunted by Ms. Green's sister's ghost!

I only have one picture of her when she was young, probably sixteen or seventeen. She's sitting cross-legged in a field of wild flowers, wearing a purple shirt and overalls. She has a beautiful big grin on her face and a gorgeous long brown braid over her shoulder. And sometimes, when I'm braiding my own hair, out of the corner of my eye, I'll catch her face in the mirror.

I went to look for that picture the other day and I couldn't find it. But I'm not worried. Sandi always turns up sooner or later.

# Part 3: Triumph
## *How We Thrive*

How do women succeed in a culture that is rife with misogyny and toxic masculinity? It certainly helps to have a strong sense of identity, and purpose. It helps to know who you are and what you're on this planet to do. But always there are obstacles to overcome, challenges to face, and heartbreaks to endure. It's the story of our lives.

FST!ers don't sugarcoat their stories or downplay the difficulties that they have faced. Telling true stories means sharing what's real, and sometimes what's real is really far from a pretty picture. What you'll never hear in a FST! story is a woe-is-me pity party. Our stories may have trauma and pain in them, but trauma and pain are never the whole story. The whole story isn't just about how we survive… it's about how we thrive.

## "Never Say Never" December 2013

"What did you take?"

"What?"

"What did you take, you need to tell us."

"I haven't taken anything."

"Look, we're not going to judge you, we just need to know."

"I haven't taken anything, I don't do drugs. I have a neurological disorder."

"Really, what do you have?"

"I actually don't know."

"Uh huh, sure, hey! Open your eyes, open your eyes! Hey, stay with us! What did you take? Nah, she's out, just another party girl."

This was a scene that got played out with paramedics in the back of many ambulances throughout my twenties. Party girl. Drug seeker. That's how the doctors and nurses would describe me when someone would bring into the ER unconscious, in debilitating pain, paralyzed, convulsing, unable to speak or communicate. If only they would check my records, they would see that I'd been here many times before.

They would see my do not resuscitate order to authorize the emergency surgery after an MRI evidenced the tumor-like mass lodged under the left side of my brain. They would see the results of my MRI, which I only had done because of a chance encounter with friend's father, who happened to be a doctor, who happened to pull colleagues' strings to get me treated.

145

That MRI should have happened years before, but because I was young with the symptoms I was presenting, they assumed I was a drug addict. Because I was poor, I didn't have the right insurance for the scans. In a moment of brutal honesty an EMT actually told me that the reason nobody was taking me seriously because I was nobody's wife, I was nobody's mother, and anybody who called me daughter wasn't there. To the medical "professionals," I was of nobody's concern. As I went in and out of hospitals for all those years, being of nobody's concern was something I began to deeply internalize. I felt it that night, being in that ambulance, a place I swore years earlier I would never be again. Damn. Never say never.

I never thought the stage for my twenties would be set with crash carts, hospitals, and doctors' offices. I always imagined the scenery would look a little different. I envisioned concert halls, classrooms, and conference tables. I was a double major in dance and English Literature in university because, clearly, I never had any aspirations to make money. When I signed my first will at twenty-two, I had offers in two international dance companies and glowing letters of recommendation to start my graduate program.

But I had to fight like hell just to get my bachelor's degree. It took years extra cutting through the red tape of medical withdrawals and incompletes. And although the initial surgery helped save my life, many of the symptoms still persisted. Yet there I was, foolishly starting my graduate degree out of state, desperately clinging to the future I had originally mapped out.

And I wouldn't leave, no way, not when my hands turned purple or even when I was teaching and I would black out, not knowing where I was. No, the point of no return came one day when I was editing a doctoral dissertation and I watched in fascinated terror as the words on the page rose up, flipped around, and reversed themselves. I remember slamming my hands down onto the pages, trying to get them to stop, trying to somehow make them go back together. It was only then that I said, "Alright, that's it, I give. You win, powers that be. I am out of here."

The words on the page wouldn't go back the same, not for a long time. By the time I got home to Tucson, I had lost 75 percent of the mobility in my arms and hands. I was becoming paralyzed. As a dancer, for whom movement is a way of life, I never thought I would have to learn how to run again. As an academic, who trades in words, I never thought I would have to learn how to read and speak well again.

Your world becomes small when your once-busy thoughts are reduced to only—Move. Your. Legs. When the ability to make a fist seems so unattainable that it is the only thing you can focus on for days. A year of intensive, excruciating physical therapy restored most of my limbs' functionality, but inconsistent aftercare, experimental treatments, and service as a pharmaceutical guinea pig had taken their toll. By the time a friend literally carried me across the border to Mexico to get the brain scan I knew I desperately needed, the blackouts and seizures struck every other day, and I was almost unconscious.

I could barely keep my head up as the doctor read me the test results back. "Well," he said, "There's absolutely nothing wrong with you."

"What?"

"Other than the fact that you are completely screwed. You have a very sick head."

"Well, tell me something I don't know, Doc."

"No, no, your brain is sick."

In five minutes, that doctor was able to do what no doctor had done in five years—explain. The tumor/mass under my brain had actually eaten away at the skull bone and leaked in. I didn't know earlier because I received no post-op care. Having it go unchecked for so long had caused so much intracranial pressure that my brain had begun short-circuiting. And it was beginning to shut down.

"Think of the brain like a computer," the doctor said. "When it short-circuits, it begins to turn off. When your electricity levels get too low, they spike, causing electrical surges in all different areas of the brain. This is why you're convulsing; this is why you're having seizures and your speech and motor skills are... loco. Your electricity level should be between 8 and 15. Yours is a 2. You're having a hard time staying awake because you're going into a coma."

"Sh... it. Okay, what's the fix, what's the cure?"

"Oh," he said, "There is none, this is why you're screwed."

In the next moment I met the series of nevers that dictated the next six years of my life. You will never be able to survive without medication to regulate your brain. You will never be as active as you once were or have much of a social life because your brain can't handle stress of any kind. You will never be able to go back to school. "Basically," he said, "You will never be normal again."

While the medication regimen I was put on kept the electricity in my brain on, it did very little to regulate it, leaving me with a regularly malfunctioning brain. This leads to a grab bag of neurological fun! Muscle spasms and grand mal seizures are one thing, but that's not even the entertaining part. Broca's aphasia and Weirneke's seizures are where some of the real fun is. I would often lose my ability to process or produce language. Sounds wouldn't register as discernable speech and there were times I wouldn't be able to form words. I had difficulty with facial recognition often not being able to recognize close friends. There were times I would suddenly not be able to recognize where I was and get lost in my own neighborhood. This made interacting with the outside world far more of a challenge.

I tried to be social and maintain a sense of normalcy, but I began living in a constant state of fear and anxiety—not knowing if the next episode meant permanent paralysis or more erasure of my long term memory. I grew accustomed to the physical pain, but I began to buckle under the psychological torment that comes with being a prisoner in your own body. And I started to become—different. Pain changes you. Fear changes you. Not being able to trust your own body to perform the simplest of tasks changes you. I became less self-assured, less confident in everything I did. I became quiet and shrank into the background more, not trusting my own voice. I contributed less to conversations because I was embarrassed by my stutter. I hid my illiteracy from my very brilliant friends. And there was a serious crisis of self occurring because, if I wasn't Mel-the-dancer or Mel-the-academic, who was I? I was becoming this nameless thing that was destroying me from the inside out. I was Mel-who-was-just-sick. And with every seizure, my resolve weakened.

And there I was one night, in the middle of a horrible episode that had left me bedridden for days. Despite too many sleeping pills, I was still wide awake. This was really dangerous because not sleeping meant my brain ran down, the seizures increased in frequency and intensity, and, with every grand mal, I risked more permanent damage.

Even before the initial surgery, when things were really bad, I would often do check-ins with myself. I'd ask myself, "Do you want to keep fighting this? If you make it through, is the quality of life you can expect going to be worth it?" I couldn't cry anymore that night. I was in so much pain and so exhausted. I went to the mirror and began my check-in. "Do you want to keep fighting this?"

And then all of the nevers I had heard over the years came together in unceremonious concert. You will never be able to go back to school. You will never be able to work full time. You will never dance again. You will never have children. You will never find a partner in this life because people say in sickness and in health, but they do so knowing they likely won't have to cross that bridge for decades. No one signs up for it initially. You will be alone, a shell of everything you thought you would or could be and living a half-life in and out of hospitals.

I looked down at the row of pill bottles in front of me and I opened them and started taking them all handful by handful. And I looked in the mirror at the shattered, hopeless girl staring back at me, who never thought this would be her life, and I asked her, "Are you sure?" And then those doctors' words rang out: You will never be normal again. And the last thing I heard was the girl in the mirror say, "I'm sorry, I can't do this anymore, I'm so sorry."

Hope is a very dangerous thing to lose. There is no cocktail of medicine more effective—no force on this earth more powerful than hope, and there is nothing more destructive than its absence. I don't remember charcoal or my stomach being pumped. What I do remember after waking up in the hospital is the nurse, upon hearing how much I took, say, "Holy shit?! You took enough to put down live-stock!"

Then she said something funny. She said, "You know something, you're a lucky, girl." "Lucky," I thought. Now there's a funny word to describe my situation. But you know what, she was right. I did get lucky that night. I got so lucky that the girl in the mirror broke. I needed her to break, she had to break. There is beauty in the breakdown because, with as many pills as I took, I never should have woken up. But I did. Which got me thinking for the first time—maybe all those other nevers weren't absolute either.

It was then that I stopped listening to never and started listening to myself again, finding my own voice. I knew the medications' side effects were causing more harm than good and I resolved then and there, against all medical advice, to get off the meds. I was determined to find a way to beat this and heal my brain and heal my body. I went to ridiculous lengths. I moved to a foreign country to get better medical care. I went through a year and a half of nightmarish, horrible withdrawals, but I was not going to let someone else's nevers be mine anymore. And it worked. I have been seizure medication-free for more than two years. And this is healthiest I've been in more than a decade.

My brain still gets run down, but I've learned to accept my limitations with grace. I'll still have seizures, but they are nowhere near the extent they once were, and I know it's only a temporary state. There are those rare times I don't recognize even close friends' faces, but now I say, "Hey, I make new friends every day and they're already really happy to meet me."

I've had to make my peace with not having the perfect future and fancy education I clung to with such vigor and destructive determination. I take comfort in knowing my survival degree program has taught me things I might not have otherwise learned. Patience, tenacity, knowing the importance of never giving up your own voice. Learning how to not give in to the fear. Understanding the importance of honoring your past, but not allowing yourself to be defined by it. Accepting your body for the incredible journey it's been on, instead of focusing imperfections and limitations. And, above all, knowing the importance of surrounding yourself with really incredible people. Hold tight to your friends and those who become your "family." If they're anything like mine, they might just be your reasons for fighting, even when you don't think you have any left.

Whatever your struggles may be, do not let somebody else's nevers become your own. Because there is only one never you should ever internalize. There is always hope. Never give up.

# FST! Tiara Bertram
## "Fish Out of Water" March 2016

If I wrote an autobiography, it could totally be called "Fish Out Of Water." I'm a Black girl who spends most of her time in predominantly White spaces. If that's not a fish out of water, I don't know what is.

I was born in a city in upstate New York, grew up in the hood on the south west side. However, my mom, who is the most fervent Christian woman I have ever met, didn't want my siblings and I to get caught up in "the things of this world" and rarely let us interact with any of the residents on the block for fear of us losing our souls if we listened to "that gangsta rap."

We used to go to the City School District. As with many urban school districts, our school was referred to by a number rather than a name. It was underfunded and many of the students were dealing with difficult home situations and would act out in class. The teachers were exhausted. My older sibling got bullied a lot and my younger sibling got in trouble for being hyperactive. So my mom enrolled us in the Urban Suburban program, which was an initiative to take students of color who had potential and send them to one of the school districts in the surrounding suburbs. The Canal Side Central School District had just opened up to the program the year we had enrolled, and so I started the 4th Grade at Hilltop Elementary School.

That first day of school was the first time I left the fishbowl. While up to that point I had known I was Black, it was the first time in my seven years of life that I truly felt "other" for being the only Black kid in the room.

I was fortunate enough that Canal Side School District is really big on having a good community. They even created a local holiday, "CARE Week." CARE stands for Civility, Awareness, Respect, and Embrace. So I didn't actually face a whole lot of blatant racism. I had this one math teacher in ninth grade, when I was taking honors geometry, and she kept treating me like I was stupid. Like she was really nice about it, asking the class if anyone had any questions at all or needed her to slow down at all, and then stared at me for like five minutes straight. Because obviously little Black girls can't be good at math. But then I was one of two students who got a perfect 100 on her midterm, so I think I showed her.

But other than that, I didn't really face people outright hating me. What I did end up with were a lot of micro-aggressions: the comments about the size of my Black booty; how the reason I can dance is because I'm Black; the surprise that my parents are more or less happily married, and all of my siblings and I were born in wedlock to thirty year old adults, not to teenagers. Don't even get me started on hair touching. In my music theory class in high school, one of my best friends stuck objects in my afro, pencils and things of the like, to see how many she could get in before I noticed.

Now here's the thing: when you spend a lot of time around people, you tend to take on their perspective. Even though the point of Urban Suburban was to change how people of color are viewed, what ended up happening was that it changed how I viewed Blackness, because my own Blackness was constantly invalidated. I didn't listen to "ghetto music." I wasn't obsessed with name brand shoes. I "talked White." One friend's mom actually told me I was "the Whitest Black girl" that she knew.

This constant binary of what all of my White friends expected Blackness to be, and the fact that I didn't fit it, actually caused me to doubt my own Blackness. And then I was mad at myself for having this identity crisis, because I wasn't even biracial so I didn't think I had a legitimate reason to feel the way I felt. I am fully, buys-foundation-that's-the-color-of-Nutella, capital-B Black.

As crazy as it sounds, this insecurity had affected the way I treated other Black people my age. Now, I'm totally comfortable with the older women at the Black churches I went to growing up. Black adults have ALWAYS loved me, because my mom has raised us to be hard working and excellent at everything we do and to respect our elders. But I was actually really scared of being rejected by my Black peers.

It's not like I can just turn myself Blacker. I had actually tried that.

153

When I attempt to speak African American Vernacular English, I literally sound like a moron, because it's so forced. So even though there were like, ten of us in the whole school, I would avoid the other Black kids that I rode the bus with because I was worried they wouldn't accept me for not being Black enough.

It was somewhat easy to avoid them anyway since I didn't actually have a whole lot of opportunities to interact with them. I didn't see them in class because I was the only one who was in all honors classes from fourth grade through most of high school. Everyone sleeps on the bus in the morning since we had to get picked up while it was still dark to make the thirty minute bus ride to Canal Side from the city, and after school I was involved in very "White" things like the Christian club, international club, theater, and mostly White sports like field hockey and tennis. (The theater thing was REALLY funny, because my high school put on a production of To Kill A Mockingbird and I was the only person who auditioned for the role of Calpurnia. The guy who played Tom Robinson didn't even audition; he was recruited by the English teacher. Because you cannot do To Kill A Mockingbird with a White Tom Robinson.)

I identified myself as the "Disney Token Black Girl" of my friends. The Disney Token Black Girl is a clearly defined role. She provides the punchline to every joke. She's fully integrated into mainstream White culture, but still sassy and loud and "eccentric," yet not "Black" enough to be threatening to her White peers (except when her "angry, violent nature" is called for, such as being willing to fight the guy who broke the White best friend's heart). But above all, the Disney Token Black Girl is an acceptable version of a Black person in a White space. So I embraced that stereotype because it was one that I could easily fit into.

I thought that would change when I went to college. I was going to the University of Arizona, where there are almost 50,000 students, so by sheer numbers there should be more Black people. However, Arizona is still a pretty White space. I was in the honors college and lived in Yuma Hall, the smaller honors dorm, so I was the only Black girl on my floor. There was another Black girl in the hall but she was really shy and no one really knew her, whereas I was loud and always in the common spaces and you can actually see the door to my room from the front desk. I was an environmental science major when I started, and I didn't have a whole lot of Black kids in my classes. I joined a campus youth group, and there was one Black girl already there but she was a junior, so I figured I would just be her successor. (Yes, I actually thought that.) So I was still in mostly White spaces, still being the Disney Token Black Girl.

Sophomore year, I tried to join one of the Black sororities. I figured it doesn't get much Blacker than that, right? But at all the events I went to, I still felt out of place, like I didn't belong. They were like these drop dead gorgeous, athletic, intelligent, classy women, and still were "authentically" Black. Like the Kerry Washingtons and Kelly Rowlands of UA. Meanwhile I felt more like a 2000's era That's So Raven. Plus, Greek life is really expensive. I ended up not joining.

My view on Blackness changed junior year, when I switched my major and did an internship for African American Student Affairs in my spring semester. I started meeting all kinds of Black people. I found Black girls who were engineering majors, Black girls who were vegetarian, I even found Black girls who liked Taylor Swift music! I didn't know that was allowed! I didn't know that there could be so much diversity within a group that is tagged as diversity itself.

I also didn't know that being Black does not mean I have to be delegated to being a secondary character in the performance that is human society. Black people are three-dimensional, real, emotional, capable people, with a right to personal agency, and to personal space. I am allowed to be offended by people constantly touching my head like I'm an alpaca at a petting zoo. I am allowed to be angry at the same system that I'm trying to navigate as I try to figure out what I want to do with my life. My standard Black women role models, Michelle Obama and Claire Huxtable, are not exceptions to Blackness.

I didn't know that I belonged, that I can claim my Blackness proudly and not be seen as a poser just because I also meet societal standards of attainment and ambition set by and usually monopolized by Whites.

I didn't know that I am authentically Black.

There's more than just one type of fish. It doesn't have to just be tuna to be fish. There's salmon, carp, bass, tilapia, goldfish, Nemo. Being different from what White society tells me I should be (and then simultaneously hates) doesn't make me any less Black.

Fish can't be out of water for long periods of time. They suffocate and die. I didn't even know I was suffocating until I submerged myself in my own culture, and met different people who were like me. That's why it's so important to have things like affirmative action, Black History Month, and the Black Lives Matter movement. This is why it's monumental that I can say my PRESIDENT is Black, for Beyoncé to be proud of our Jackson 5 nostrils and say we slay! We can't breathe if we're constantly choking on negative messages.

I've learned to recognize that Blackness comes in a lot of different shades, careers, and interests. So I ask you, reader, to help us spread our self-love. Remember that speaking properly is not restricted to Whites. Curly hair is not unprofessional. There's more death happening in the Black community besides Black bodies being shot down for no reason. We're killed in our dreams and ambitions, in how we're perceived, in how we're defined.

We all know dead fish stink, so stop killing us and making things stink.

## FST! Charli Swinford
## "A Word of Advice" January 2015

Three years ago, I accepted a job running a non-profit in St. Louis Missouri. It seemed like an amazing opportunity—other than that whole "moving to Missouri" thing. Yeah, complicated. But I can handle complicated. Just to frame this, I am a big fan of air travel—I get on board, have a cocktail, take a nap, someone else flies the damn plane and, boom, a couple hours later, life returns to normal. With that in mind, I called Southwest Airlines (if I was going to move my entire life, their "bags fly free" policy was going to save me a fortune.) Sadly, they informed me, in no uncertain terms, that a Mazda Miata cannot be brought on the plane as carry-on baggage; in fact, it cannot be checked baggage either. There is no grey area in this policy, at all. It is a really small car, but not baggage small. Thus I had no choice but to drive.

To that end, I packed my entire life into and onto a 2003 Mazda Miata—yes that is possible... really... I'm a minimalist, I hate owning stuff... seriously I did this. All packed, I set off on a roughly 1500 mile road trip by myself—it's a Miata, you can bring stuff or a passenger, not both. An estimated 25 hours of driving, across five states, one woman, alone... I got this. So, I set my alarm for bright and early. The idea was to hit the road about 5 a.m., or, you know, 10:30—these things never seem to go as planned. No problems, I can make up time across the wide open desert. A quick slide across the bottom of Arizona and off into New Mexico. I've always had a sneaking love of New Mexico, which was a good thing, because I was going to be there a long time. Beautiful state—but it never ends. If you drive Interstate 10 to US 70, it is 475 miles across New Mexico on an angle. Interesting ride. You get to see White Sands, Alamo Gordo, Roswell, a whole lot of nothing in between... but scenic nothing.

I bypassed Roswell. For all the talk, it's basically an overblown trailer park full of tourists that harbor paranoid fantasies about aliens. I'm from Tucson—if I want to experience a paranoid trailer park I can

157

go to Flowing Wells. Sure, the paranoia is meth induced and doesn't involve aliens, but that's kind of a nitpicky distinction. I point this out not for the benefit of that joke, but to foreshadow the fuel crisis I was about to have.

About 90 miles north of Roswell lays Portales, NM—there is nothing in between. Portales is the peanut capital of the Southwest… everybody has to be proud of something. I slid into peanut town on fumes, hungry, and needing a restroom. It was about 7 p.m. and almost dark. Not much is open in Portales at 7 p.m.—or ever, near as I can tell. My only option for my needs was Allsups. For those unfamiliar, Allsups is kind of like Circle K—except it is filthy, poorly stocked, and sucks in all discernable ways. I made a bee-line for the restroom, which was, of course, out of order. Not good. So I grabbed some snacks and got in line to pre-pay for my fuel. Peanut farming apparently creates powerful levels of thirst, because there were about ten people in front of me, all carrying 30 packs of cheap, canned, domestic beer. Swell people, and they really seemed to like me—by which I mean, the lone Trans woman in the rural gas station was contemplating how long she had before walking upright and breathing became a thing of the past. I pumped the car full and got the hell out of town, holding my legs together tightly and praying my bladder held.

About 20 miles North of Portales is Clovis, New Mexico—the dairy capital of the Southwest, in case you were keeping track of these things. And, thank goddess, another Allsups, this one with a working restroom… filthy, but working. Just a quick stop this time, restroom only. I wanted another soda for the road, but I wasn't queueing up in the "rednecks from hell buying cheap beer" line again (dairy farming seems to also make people crave bad beer). A quick ride east and, FINALLY, the Texas state line.

The Texas panhandle is about as dull as a Baptist church picnic—it's Kansas with more cowboy hats. Dead flat, dark, and barren. Mind you, I am over 600 miles into this trip. There is a point where the road gets to you, when the hours sink in, the body aches begin, and the Red Bull wears off. An almost surreal state of fatigue, you've become a

158

road zombie. I was contemplating that, and to be honest, trying to chain smoke my way through it, when in the distance appeared a shocking blast of green neon.

What on earth could this be? Did the Roswell aliens blow their landing coordinates? And how much are they going to hate this barren patch of hell? As I got closer, the smell became overpowering – I grew up in the Midwest, I know cows when I smell them—but this was a much stronger smell, and my mind was too shot to contemplate what the hell cows had to do with neon.

Then the words written big in green neon became clear: Cargill Meats. I was driving through the largest cattle feed lot I have ever seen, and someone thought it wise to provide neon signage for the future hamburgers. I'm not sure how they felt about that, but it kinda flipped me the hell out. Is there an old bull out there pulling calves aside? "Listen kid, don't trust the big green light, cows flock to it, and they never return." I dunno. There was a profound thought in all of this somewhere, but it was abruptly sidetracked by lights of a different color—red and blue to be precise.

Being a queer woman, alone, out of state, driving after dark—some local yokel traffic cop was probably the last person I wanted to deal with. I grabbed my phone, called a friend and said "just keep the line open and listen, shit could get weird" and pulled over. No worries, it was just a burned out license plate light. I know this for a fact because it took two hours and every on-duty police officer in Bovina, Texas to explain it to me. Well, one officer and five minutes would have sufficed—but apparently I am the kind of novelty that needed to be shared with co-workers. There's a feel good. Normally I have a bit of an attitude problem about that shit, but it occurred to me that if I piss off an entire rural police force and they decide to retaliate… well… who exactly the hell would I call for help? No, this was a time to play nice and smile politely.

No tickets, which is fortunate because driving with a burned out license plate lamp in Texas can really be a lot of trouble—maybe even a felony. I'm not sure on that, but the one officer was very insistent that I not drive onward until tomorrow morning—I guess the police in the next town are a lot less friendly. Fortunately, there is a hotel right on the edge of the next town, and an auto parts store a few blocks from the hotel. He was even willing to call ahead and hold a room for me, and offered to stop by in the morning to fix my lighting issue.

On the one hand, this was arguably the most terrifying moment of my life. On the other hand, I saw a crack in the door. "Why yes, thank you officer (said with an overplayed flirtatious smile). You are so nice. Go ahead and have a room held for me, I would hate to have problems up the road." He called the hotel, gave me back my license, and said he would stop by in an hour or so to make sure I made it safely (yes, he went there). I smiled and pulled back onto the road, driving slow and steady as the headlights of his still parked squad car slowly faded. I crossed over a small rise, saw the hotel just coming into view… dropped my foot to the damn floor and didn't stop until Oklahoma. GONE! No hotel, no nice evening with officer psycho, I ain't even stopping for gas in this god forsaken state.

(As an aside—leaving a phone call going for two hours is really a big battery drain. Of course, the 12 volt charger was nowhere to be found—is it ever? I wasn't stopping in Texas to look for it, and I was terrified by the idea of not having a phone just at that moment. Improvisation time—the laptop is on the passenger seat, the USB cables are in the laptop bag. So, here I am blasting across the Texas panhandle at 100 miles an hour, with my laptop open on the passenger seat for the sole purpose of charging my phone, while chain smoking and crying my eyes out in terror and rage. Talk about road trips you won't soon forget.)

Western Oklahoma, in case you were wondering, is basically Texas, except they cheer for different college football teams. Not my idea of safety. Despite my exhaustion, this would be a fuel and Red Bull stop only (and thank Goddess it wasn't another Allsup's). I did get harassed by a cop for using the ladies room—if you see an incredibly ugly pattern forming here, were on the same page.

Back on the road, back on the throttle, looking for civilization or something like it. I finally shut down at about 4 a.m., at a Motel 6 on the north side of Oklahoma City. The desk clerk hit on me, Jimmy the pimp rolled up in his Lexus to drop off a couple of girls, the streets were way too busy for 4 a.m., but despite the bustle, absolutely nothing legal was transpiring. This was the safest I had felt in hours. I took comfort in knowing that I would be left alone, not visited by sleaze balls with badges, and since Jimmy the pimp had seen my bags he knew I wasn't local so not a threat. I slept like a baby.

A word of advice? Stay on your toes and assume nothing. Sometimes the pimps are less threatening than the cops. Sometimes the inviting neon lights are just a slaughterhouse. Sometimes the FAA baggage regulations are a big pain. Sometimes the restrooms are out of order. Life is a lot like being up here on stage—you  script it out, rehearse it to death, and when the lights come up… you improv like a mad woman.

Cat Belue
## "What a Disaster" February 2015

I don't know why, but it seems to me like most of the biggest disasters in history involved water. The biblical flood, the Titanic, Hurricane Katrina, and mine and Jenny's first big date.

See, we had known each other for over a year as friends but when we started dating, everything changed. Suddenly there's a desire to impress this person and you find yourself saying "Yes" to things you'd never consider in your normal brain.

So when Jenny asked me if I liked to go canoeing, I gave a resounding "YES"! Now technically, I had been in a canoe. Once. It was in a pond about the size of an Olympic pool with no current and it was only a couple feet deep. So clearly I felt up to the challenge. She suggested we sign up for the sort of canoe trip where the rental company drives you, the canoe and whatever supplies you bring a few miles upstream then drop you and leave you on your own.

I was nervously excited as the "tour guide" loaded us into the single bench seat of his 70's model Ford rust bucket F-150 as the three of us sat crowded together for the drive. Being in the South, for a moment I braced myself for the sound of a banjo but the moment passed and we were on our way. As we rattled our way up the dirt trail suddenly the trees cleared to my left and I got a good view of the rushing river paralleling us. WTF?? Rushing Water?! As casually as I could without letting my voice sound as panicked as I felt, I asked, "That's not what we're going to be canoeing in is it?"

"Yeah, all this rain has the crik up a bit I reckon," he said.

Creek? Hell, this was a river if ever I'd seen one and it was now starting to look like a scene from Deliverance!

"Y'all ladies good swimmers?" he asked.

Jenny nodded yes. I didn't say anything. I was too busy surveying the rocky terrain we were flying over to see where I was going to land when I jumped out of the truck.

"We've had a kayak and canoe get tumpt over this morning, the kayak ain't been found yet so y'all be careful. About a mile down from the drop point, there's a big split in the water and you wanna stay left. Stay LEFT! And paddle fast. Don't go to the right, you'll get sucked in, that's what happened to them others."

As we came to a stop, he unloaded our gear and, as he was pulling away, he said "Alrighty then, good luck and we'll see back at the pullout when you get there."

And like that he was gone. I watched the truck pulling away and it was all I could do to not ditch out on Jenny and run after him like the scared little bitch I was. But then I remembered—I was falling in love, and that feeling gives you mad courage like nothing else can. So I swallowed back the bile, steadied my shaking hands, put on an "I'm cool" face, and, with canoe in one hand, cooler in the other, we set off towards the ever increasing roar of liquid thunder.

Let me offer you some background story here: I had gotten to know Jenny pretty good by this time from hanging out with our group of friends. I had been in a pool and at the beach with her and knew that she was like a sexy aquatic mammal, perfectly at home in the water. I, however, was a lumbering land dweller that preferred to hug the side of the pool at the 4-foot depth. And always with a beer and cigarette in my hands so it looked like I was just chilling out, instead of exposing myself as someone unable to swim.

So when we pushed off from the bank into the current, I felt about as comfortable as a goldfish in a blender. But as we started down the river, I found that it wasn't near as bad as it had looked or sounded. As a matter of fact, it was rather calm and we quickly fell into a nice cadence of rowing. I felt silly for ever having been worried; I figured the sound must have been amplified by the trees and wind. It was a gorgeous, sunny November day, clear blue skies and in the high 60's. It was so warm that when we pulled into a covey for a picnic lunch, we stripped down to our swimsuits and crawled up on a big rock to enjoy our wine... yes, I know I'm a staunch beer drinker... and cheese... not a big fan... but hey, the things we do right? We sat there till we finished off the wine, talking, laughing and flirting, then with a bit of a buzz we climbed back into the canoe and headed back to the pullout.

I think I had fallen into a sort of lull until I heard what sounded like the bowels of hell opening wide. As we rounded a bend in the water we both saw the great split at the same time. There were huge rocks and broken tree parts littering the center of the path and a clearly delineated left and right side. "Left! Go left!", we both yelled as we dug our paddles into the murky water. Our speed had intensified as the current flung us forward, faster and faster. We were dodging the boulders and debris as well as we could as our canoe rocked and smashed its way begrudgingly towards the left. The sound of the crashing water was deafening and I couldn't hear what Jenny was saying, I was just concentrating on paddling left with all my might.

Suddenly as we careened off yet another huge rock I saw the waterfall we were bearing down on and it was too late to do anything other than brace for the impact. As our canoe went first up then over the 6 foot drop we came to a swift and immediate stop as the front end wedged between two boulders. I watched as my shorts that I'd removed earlier went flying over my head and disappeared in the frothy swirl ahead, never to be seen again. Somehow, we and the rest of our supplies stayed in the canoe but water was pouring in soaking everything. We were both visibly shaken so we just sat there for a minute.

"Are you okay?" I asked.

"Yeah, I think so, you?"

"Yeah" "What the hell?! That dyslexic hillbilly must have meant his other left! Now what?" I asked.

"We've got to get out of the boat and try to push it off the rocks."

165

Jenny said.

I just stared at her and wondered who in the world she was talking to. I knew that I was perfectly prepared to stay in the boat until the helicopters came to save us.

"Come on!" she said, as she climbed out and into the freezing cold water.

I continued to sit there, hoping that by some miracle everything would unhappen. It didn't.

"Come on, this water's cold, you need to get out and help me free the canoe."

Fear was trying to win out but thankfully rational thought reminded me that we really had no other option. There was no telling if or when another boat might come along and no way of knowing how far we were from the pullout. Finally, reluctant as all hell, I left the safety of the boat and joined Jenny in the frigid water.

The sheer force of the water made it difficult to stand upright. We unloaded the cooler and perched it on top of the rocks and I held it with one hand and worked to free the canoe with the other. Dressed only in swimsuits and tennis shoes, our feet and legs were going numb. After several long hard minutes the canoe finally gave loose, and promptly took off without us! Without hesitation Jenny jumped into the coursing whirlpool after it while I stood there open-mouthed. She caught up to it, managed to climb in and rowed herself to shore.

The noise from the rapids made it nearly impossible to hear her but I could see clearly what she was doing. She had opened the backpack and was attempting to light a cigarette…from a pack that was actively draining water, with a lighter that had been submerged the entire time. I watched as she frantically struck at the Bic, the soggy cigarette bending under the weight of the sopping wet tobacco. Meantime while I stood in the waist deep freezing water, holding on to the cooler and trying not to drown, I knew that if the tables were turned,

I'd be doing the same thing! Of course, she soon realized her efforts were futile and now she had to contend with what to do with me.

She dumped the water out of the canoe, climbed in and started to work her way upstream toward me. It took great effort to fight the current and when she got close enough I managed to throw the cooler into the boat because you know, priorities. Now there was just me. "You're going to have to jump in the water and swim to shore", she says.

I looked at the churning water, the jump over all the jagged rocks and the distance to shore and shook my head "NO" vigorously.

"You have to!"

Nope, no, no way, not happening, I'll stay here till I die from natural causes but I am not jumping to my own death.

"You can swim, right?"

The question hung in the air like an accusation.

"Not really," I mumbled. It occurred to me that my impress-o-meter was dipping precariously into the negative.

"Well, I'll get as close as I can and you're going to have to jump into the canoe." Jenny said.

Holy shit. She made a mad dash towards me but the current pushed her back out. She dug in and tried again but before she was close enough the boat got swept back out. Right about now I'm thinking I wish I had a burlier girlfriend! I mean sexy, aquatic mammal isn't helping me now, I need some damn muscles!

"You're going to have to climb further out on the rocks" she yelled.

Further out was not of interest to me as the rocks were really slippery, but I realized I was going to have to in order to have a shot at making it. It was on about the fourth attempt and according to her the last one she had the strength to make, when I finally summoned the courage to take a flying leap… landing awkwardly but safely into the canoe.

Freezing and shaken, exhausted and exhilarated, we continued down river to realize that we had only been about a five-minute trip away from getting help. As we paddled up to the shoreline at the pullout Jenny didn't wait to ditch out of the still moving boat. Unfortunately, her forward momentum resulted in pushing the boat, with me still in it, back toward the current. "Hey!" I yelled and she turned in time to grab the oar I was extending and pull me back to terra firma.

Half-naked, soaked and freezing, we made our way past the obvious stares of the guys at the pullout with as much pride as we could muster. We sloughed our way to the car when there were dry clothes and most importantly, dry smokes.

So, while it was a bit of a disaster, we learned that neither of us panicked. We worked as a team, well, mainly Jenny worked, but I stayed right there on that rock so she knew where I was and I think that's important to build that kind of trust in a relationship. We had survived to row another day!

## FST! Nöel Hennessey
## "Never Say Never" December 2013

I've been a runner for as long as I can remember. My dad, my little brother Patrick, and I would run around our neighborhood on Saturday mornings when I was a kid. I wore pink and purple windbreaker pants with a matching jacket, and my brother wore a red sweat suit, and we'd trail behind my father and repeat after him as he yelled call-and-response-style songs from his Army days.

I look back now and realize that these songs were full of references to booze and the objectification of women—I wonder if the neighbors thought it was distasteful to have young children participating in these chants, or if maybe they thought it was funny or cute? Realistically, I think they were relieved to see us outside being active with our father. Maybe, if they knew our family, they'd feel some sense of relief that, since two of us were running through the neighborhood chanting about cocaine, that meant my mom only had half of her four children under foot at the house. In any case, my relationship with running started in childhood.

In high school, I ran on the track team. I ran for three years, and my senior year I finished high school with a state championship. It was my last day of high school, and also the most memorable. I was so excited about our surprise victory—we slipped into the state rankings the last few weeks of the season, then beat the first place team by over 12 seconds on race day—and also so relieved that high school track was over.

I had sweat, vomited, cried, and soaked in ice baths for this team, and I arrogantly told my coach that for the rest of my life I was never running again unless I was running late. I remember Coach Blumenstein looking at me, very seriously and maternally saying, "I really hope that's not true. Running is something you can do for the rest of your life."

Coach Blumenstein proved a wise sage. I really did love to run, I just didn't want to run for her. So I kept running in college. I clear my head and de-stress or avoid studying. Running to avoid studying became my most beloved activity in college. I also ran to recover from hangovers, which was my third most beloved activity. Second obviously goes to getting plastered. Sometimes I combined those pastimes by running from bar to bar in the winter months to keep warm.

After I graduated from college, I moved to Tucson. I quickly discovered Reid Park, the mecca of non-extreme exercise enthusiasts in central Tucson, and I frequently drove there after work to see how fast I could run around the loop. I didn't have much and I didn't know a lot of people, and running at Reid Park was my constant. I wasn't a new person in Tucson without friends or money when I was running—I was the same person who chanted with my dad running around our neighborhood, who competed in track in high school, and who avoided outside responsibilities with light jogs in college.

A lot changed for me when I moved to Tucson, though. About a month after moving here, I started the most toxic part of my life without even realizing that anything had changed.

I started dating a guy, even though something deep inside me kept telling me not to. I met him at work. I saw him semi-regularly in meetings—we worked in different offices. I thought he'd make a good friend; he thought we needed to be more. I wish I knew how to explain it, but the best way to say it is that he wore me down.

Eventually, it seemed like a good idea to be with him. I wanted to be with him, even though it seemed like he took up more of my time than he should. Whenever I expressed doubt about how much time we spent together, he'd say, "This is just how relationships work. I've been in more relationships than you—just trust me." At the time I couldn't see that the message was really "Don't trust your intuition. Don't trust yourself."

I stopped running so much. At first it was just because I didn't have time. I was always with him. He told me that if I wanted to stay in shape, I should just learn the sports that he liked. I tried those and I hated them. I wasn't an athlete, I was a runner, and running wasn't just about staying in shape; it was about going someplace else, mentally. I could run for 45 minutes and just think. Growing up in a big family meant that alone time was a precious commodity, and the time I've spent running has been the only time in my life I've ever been able to just think. I could think and run and not even realize how far I had gone.

He told me that he hated that I wanted to go out running by myself, because it was dangerous. I told him Reid Park was lit up like a Christmas tree and it was crowded with people exercising, but he told me I couldn't go to Reid Park, because he might need to use my car and he didn't have one.

As the relationship progressed, running became one of many constant sources of conflict. There was always a reason why I couldn't or shouldn't do it. Looking back, it's almost farcical that he cited danger as a reason I shouldn't go run, because I was always in the most danger when I was with him.

The first time he threatened to punch me was on Valentine's Day.

Years prior in college, I had declared myself a feminist. I swore I was strong and independent and I wouldn't ever let a man push me around. That Valentine's Day I heard those words come out of his mouth and it was like trying to stop an avalanche. By the time I realized what was happening, I was halfway buried. I knew I was in too deep, and I didn't know how to get away. The words "I'd never let a man treat me like that" seemed too ridiculously simple.

The thing people never seem to understand about dating violence is the complexity of the two people involved. I didn't enter this relationship a completely confident, unscathed-by-life woman, and he didn't have a rosy, stable history either. Sometimes I look back and wish my parents hadn't hit me as a kid. I wish they didn't belittle me, call me names, tell me that I probably deserved it when I was 14 and my older brother gave me a black eye. I wish I had a voice when I was younger. I wish I knew my worth.

He dealt with his pain by controlling and belittling me, blaming any and everyone else for the things he didn't like about his life. I dealt with my pain by internalizing and believing everything he told me about how worthless and unlovable I was.

Eventually I gave up running all together. It wasn't worth the inevitable fight that I would inevitably lose. I got pretty unhealthy, physically and mentally. While I gained weight on my body, I was deteriorating emotionally. I felt weak and trapped, so I decided to run again. But this time, I knew I needed to run away.

One day, after a particularly bad argument, I told him I was leaving and I walked out the door. I opened the car door and got in. I started reversing the car, and in an act of frustration and pure impotence, he pounded his fist into the windshield.

We were both stunned when it shattered.

What I did next is something that I'll regret for a long, long time.

I stopped the car. I got out. And I screamed at him. I called him a violent asshole. I told him he needed to fix it. I demanded to know what the fuck he was thinking.

And I gave him enough time to recover from the shock and start to blame me. I got back in the car, but this time, he was fast, and he got in, too. I started to back out of our driveway but he grabbed the wheel. Our duplex was set a good 50 feet from the street, so I had time to accelerate while he physically fought me for control of the wheel.

By the time we got to the end of the driveway I had to make a choice: keep going and crash my car, or hit the brakes. A cloud of dust flew into the air as I stopped the car, and he immediately grabbed for the keys in the ignition. He grabbed the keys and I remember bringing my foot up to his wrist and physically pinning it down so that I could pull my key chain back. I remember we wrestled with so much force that the actual key ring straightened as we pulled apart my

172

cluster of keys. I had the house key, and he had the car key. He told me to go back to the house, and I did.

I sat down on the floor of our tiny bathroom, put my head on my knees, and cried. He apologized softly, and took my phone so he could call someone to repair my windshield. I wasn't stupid—he just didn't want me calling the police.

A few minutes later we saw flashlights in our window, followed by a knock on our door. One of our neighbors must have made the call.

A few minutes after that, I watched as they handcuffed someone I loved and put him in a police van. You might think I felt relief, that this was a good thing, but all I felt was powerless. And ashamed and guilty. And alone. The cops looked at me with such disgust as I cried and told them I didn't want a restraining order.

After the police left my apartment, all I had was my own neurosis and adrenaline to keep me company. I remember watching old episodes of Lost all night on Hulu. I didn't sleep at all. I didn't have a phone, but it didn't matter. I didn't have anyone to call. I deserved this Hell I was in. The next day I paid $200 to have my windshield replaced, then immediately went out to the jail to pick him up. I listened while he convinced me that this was entirely my fault. It took another year and a half to leave for real.

I faced off with him again nearly two years later across a conference table at the courthouse downtown. We were getting a divorce, and a lot had changed between us. In the last six months, we both moved out of our apartment, he had a new girlfriend, and I had a new pair of running shoes.

I started running around Reid Park again, and I started to connect to the things I wanted in life. I wanted to be athletic again. I wanted to run fast. I wanted to be happy. I wanted to compete in the races that I took for granted when I was younger. I wanted to be independent. I wanted my knees to stop hurting when I ran. I wanted to run a marathon. I wanted to do the work.

173

I wanted this divorce to be over. He moved out in March. I filed the paperwork in April and our court date was set for late October. The waiting game was excruciating, and the anxiety I felt when I thought about how terribly things could go on the day of our hearing was suffocating. Yet another attempt to run away had me feeling powerless and alone.

But I got out of bed each day. Some days this was easier than others. I talked to friends, my grandma, a therapist, a pastor. I cried. I prayed. I ran. And one day I woke up and realized that I wasn't running in place, and I couldn't believe how far I had gone. I signed up for my first half-marathon, and my weekly "long-runs" reminded me just how hard it is to be strong.

Although the words "strength" and "endurance" conjure thoughts of heroism and hope, they don't really match how I feel when I am sweaty and tired and achy and thirsty and hungry, and wondering why in the fuck am I still running after two hours. In those moments of desperation, I tried to think about the finish line for the race I was preparing for, and think about how proud and happy I would be to cross it.

I crossed the finish line of my divorce relatively unscathed.

I beat my estimated finish time for the half-marathon by about ten minutes, and ran it again a year later in under two hours. The following year, I ran a full marathon.

I realized that I never want to stop running again.

I wrote the first draft of this story before I actually completed the marathon. It's funny, because I attempted to describe what happened when I ran 26.1 miles before I actually ran 26.1 miles. I had this beautiful prose about keeping my eyes on the horizon while focusing on my form—a metaphor for looking ahead to the future while paying close attention to how I live each day. I even wrote a line about your future being that imaginary line in the horizon that recedes as you approach it—poetry about this moving target called life.

174

Here's what actually happened: Less than one mile into the marathon, during one of the more crowded periods of the race, a woman in front of me dropped some trail mix. Instead of running to the side and safely backtracking to get her snack, she turned around and ran right into me. This lady straight up clobbered me, I rolled my ankle over, and I had more than 25.5 miles to go.

I ran the rest of the race—avoiding the reality that I may have hurt myself—but I can't say I stared up at the horizon or focused on my form per my original plan. I shivered and cried and hobbled and finally crossed the finish line after about five hours, where my boyfriend awaited to congratulate and hug me.

I wish I could say that I finished that race in my goal time all while staring at the horizon and focusing on my form, but I don't think that's the real reason I'm writing this story. There's no formula for living a safe and happy existence. Sometimes I'm able to focus on my form and keep my eyes on the horizon, and other times life has clobbered me. And I never stop surprising myself with my ability to keep running and cross the finish line.

I don't have love, or marriage, or running all figured out. I think back to that last day of high school, when I declared that, "I'm never running again unless I'm running late," and I can't help but smile and shake my head and feel gratitude that I was wrong.

Never say "never"…

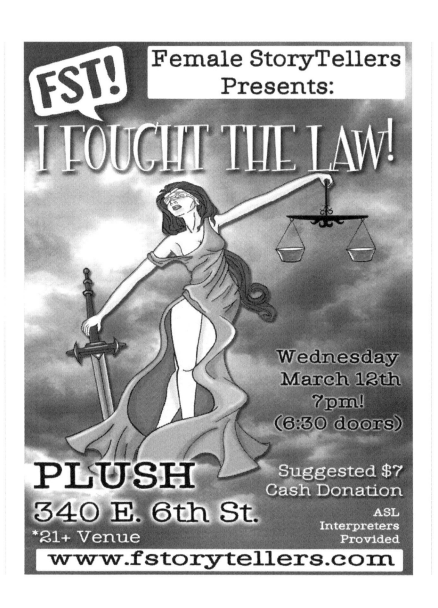

"I Fought the Law" March 2014

If you had asked me in sixth grade to name my two best friends, I would have said Harry Potter and Puppy, my pet ferret. I would not have been mistaken, either, because, they were the two friends I spent the most time with.

I had just moved to the suburban mecca of Mesa, Arizona and despite my heroic attempts to make friends, I just could not. Instead of socializing during recess, I would sit under a ramada and read The Chamber of Secrets for the fifteenth time. Instead of playing outside with neighborhood kids, I would create mazes out of boxes and toilet paper rolls for my pet ferret, Puppy—my other best friend.

While I was trying to master the art of being a loner, the truth was, I was really just lonely.

I don't remember exactly how I found the church or if the church found me. I remember I was in sixth grade and suddenly my life had changed—I had a community and a family; I had friends, I had a mentor. I had people to talk to and hang out with.

By the time I had entered high school, I spent summers at youth retreats; I became an acolyte for my church. If you don't know what an acolyte is, you're really missing out. You get to wear a white robe and light things on fire—those things being altar candles, but when you're a 13 year old church girl, you take what you can get. I taught Sunday school and I helped organize fundraisers for our church. I was the lead in several church plays and, trust me, I rocked a military uniform in a Broadway-worthy rendition of A Christmas Operation. I even ironed an elderly woman's napkins for three hours to raise money for our Lord and Savior, Jesus Christ.

But my biggest memory of the church was being confirmed. In my church, you are not a member just by going, you must go through an arduous process called Confirmation around the time you're starting high school. So every Wednesday, I spent three hours in a tiny cramped room with a dozen other high school students, studying the Small Catechism, memorizing prayers and reading the bible with our old, decrepit, very German pastor.

At 14 years old, becoming a member of our church was probably the coolest thing going on in my life. I would no longer be an extension of my parents in our church community; I would be myself. Confirmation was like the church's version of My Sweet 16. I could stand alone and be recognized in my faith as an adult, no longer a child, and that sounded really cool to me.

I didn't mind the memorization homework or the weeks of class. The fancy ceremony could not come soon enough and I took pride in creating the beautiful stoles I would wear on my special day. I would love to share pictures of this special moment in my life; unfortunately, they are all of me, kneeling in front of our pastor, with my head inches from his crotch—which, oddly enough, no one thought was weird at the time.

I had found a much-needed home in my church; a safe space for myself outside of a very stupid, dumb, and lame high school, where I could shine as the star of the play to clapping audiences and step up and be the leader I could not be anywhere else. I had gained so much from my community, and, consequently, the law of my church had become my law. It was the law I lived by.

And I took it very seriously.

It got a little hard to follow this law when I realized I had an overwhelming attraction to girls. I spent an entire Saturday night kissing a girl I met off of rainbowplanet.com in my dad's Jacuzzi, only to go to church on an hour of sleep and vow to never ever ever do again the horrible, wonderful and terribly exciting thing I had just loved doing.

I was wracked with guilt. I "knew" what I was doing was not only wrong, but somehow much worse than the "extra-curricular activities" of my heterosexual and sexually active church peers. I was breaking my own "law"—the code I had agreed to live my life by.

Secretly, I made vow after vow, broke promise after promise, to be better; to be different.

Eventually, I couldn't keep living in two worlds, pretending one did not exist while in the other. Instead of "coming out" and being asked to leave my church, I did what 95% of high school students do anyway—I just stopped going. I divorced my church before my church could divorce me. And I had the perfect excuse: college! In college, I learned about gay-straight alliances, IBT's, craigslist and OKCupid. (Those were some scholarship dollars well spent, Mom and Dad.)

But when I say that I divorced my church, I mean it felt like a divorce, a heart wrenching break-up. I was leaving the arms of a place that had once given me so much comfort. But I knew I couldn't stay in a place where I'd never be allowed to be myself.

Eight years have passed since I left that place. In that time, I took full advantage of the fact that OKCupid was free. I dated around. A lot. Six months ago, I finally struck OKCupid gold and met someone I wanted to go on more than a few dates with.

April is the type of person it is impossible to dislike. Her sense of humor, charismatic personality, and generous heart quickly convinced me to leave behind my days of trolling for dates online. In a relatively brief time, we've built a strong and committed relationship together, supporting each other's careers, passions, and interests. April also grew up in "the church"—something that immediately connected us.

When my queer friend Allison invited me to her church, I was skeptical and, for many weeks, I put the idea of attending on the backburner. But somehow, the stars aligned one Sunday. April did not have roller derby practice and when she brought up the topic of visiting the church, I put on a brave face and said, yes it did sound like the best idea ever. (I was lying.)

179

Secretly, I was mortified. I couldn't grasp going to back to church, let alone with my girlfriend. I had nightmares of being rejected at the door; being stared at, being called onto the stage to renounce my sinful lifestyle. I even considered the illusion that "Queer friend Alison" was not queer at all. Instead, the whole thing was an elaborate trick so I could be "saved" from same-sex attraction.

My guilty confession is that I didn't believe I belonged in church. There was not space for people like me. I was about to break a very serious personal law I had believed for the better part of my childhood. And I was scared shitless that I was going to get caught.

On our way to church, April barely spoke. She apologized for being so quiet—so unlike her—and explained that she was nervous. I was nervous, too, but I told her I was excited. When we parked, I took a longer than usual moment to gather my thoughts and my breath. I could feel anxiety building in my body: a knot in my chest, a lump in my throat, my hands were shaky. I was freezing and sweating simultaneously. "We only have to go once," I reassured her, "and if it sucks, we never have to come back".

We awkwardly stumbled into the church, shaking too many hands, greeting strangers too loudly in an obvious attempt to appear confident, and then sitting as quietly as possible in the back, all the way to the right, close to an exit—just in case.

We didn't touch each other, out of respect, out of fear, out of not knowing what to do at church anymore, worried that maybe we were at the wrong church and we'd be apprehended at any moment. I knew she was envisioning similar nightmares to the ones I had in my head of being rejected, of failed expectations, of not being able to reconcile our past lives with our present lives.

Service began. I saw the acolytes light the altar candles and I was reminded of the role I once had served, those children dressed in white robes and ropes tied around the waists. The format, hymns, and sermon were so familiar, I could have been at the church I grew up in.

Except, at one point, the pastor spoke about how important it was to oppose SB1062. And EVERYONE IN THE CONGREGATION CLAPPED. No, they didn't just clap; they applauded loudly and proudly—everyone in agreement—that SB1062 has no place in Arizona. Tears immediately formed in my eyes as I began to understand that I was sitting in a church, listening to a pastor say that SB1062 would not be supported by him; listening to a congregation say they could not support it either.

After service was over, we were invited to a coffee hour in the neighboring hall. We met a few people and did that church chit chat thing. Each time, April introduced me as her girlfriend and I introduced her as mine. No one batted an eye. One particularly interesting fellow, a mellow, older guy named Tom, a Tenor from the choir, sat for a minute and talked to us about the church and its history.

Eventually, April and I excused ourselves and said goodbye to Tom. Before leaving, he hugged both of us. He told us he prided himself on being the best hugger in the entire congregation.

We thanked him for being so welcoming. He paused and very intently looked at us. Slowly, he said, "Well, you ARE welcome!"

And for the first time, I believed it.

Sometimes the hardest laws we have to fight are the ones we write ourselves.

# FST! Jamie
## "Good Intentions" January 2016

I don't really recall how or why it started. Maybe it was a New Year's resolution. Did it start in 2003? 2004? Why can't I remember? I was a sophomore in college. I remember that. I remember that I had been dating this guy for several months, and that I was in love with him, and that he had something to do with it. But the specifics of when or how or why it happened have gotten lost in the shadow of the heavy shame that followed.

We decided (or maybe he decided and I just followed along) that we would start going to the gym, get fit. Neither of us were particularly unhealthy. We didn't smoke or drink. We weren't overweight. But he decided he wanted to get into body building. And I wanted to spend every waking moment with him because well, 20 year old me was in way over my head with this relationship. And besides this was going to be fun. We were going to get healthy. Seriously. That was the intention.

This is where my story ends. This is where I fall away from myself and into the trap. This is where I spiral into that oblivion of self-hate and self-deprecation, the whirlpool where so many of my sisters have been and some still are. Some never make it out. Some get sucked so far down by the riptide that they slowly, and sometimes quickly, melt away before our very eyes. And those of us who make it out are left to carry the cold weight of self-harm. And it is a heavy thing to carry. And it has worn me to my bones. But I refuse to stand in the shadow of its shame.

When you become an anorexic, you get very clever about managing appearances for the outside world. You become a 'quirky' eater to your friends. Your roommates remark, "Damn, you really like green beans, Jamie. I see you have entire cabinet full of them." Yeah, I do. They have 20 calories per serving, so I love them. I eat a can a day. That's my dinner. Sometimes I'll get crazy and put a bit of non-fat cottage cheese on top. But that's only if I've spent extra time on the cardio machines that day; I can reward myself.

It took me about a year to get really good at starving myself. At first, I didn't have the discipline. I wasn't quite ready to take control. Once I started keeping a food journal with my daily caloric intake, this changed. I could work with numbers. I could control the numbers. 1000 calories? Easy. 800? No problem. 600? You got this. And I did. 600 calories a day. I remember that number. I was so proud of myself.

I was also cold. I was always cold. It could be 90 degrees outside and I would have on a sweatshirt. It served double duty: it kept me warm and it hid my bones. No questions asked. And no questions were asked, ever, by anyone. In fact, I was celebrated, loved for the shrinking woman I became. And as my physical body got smaller and smaller, so too did my passion for life. I could see my light fading. I was dying.

Sometime into year two, my hair started falling out. I would find small little clumps on my pillow. The shower drain would be clogged up. I started noticing these little white hairs growing on my arms. It was my body's way of trying to protect itself. My body was fighting to stay alive. And no one said a word.

That's not true. Lots of people said lots of things. Things like, "Wow! You're so skinny." "Oh my god, you've lost weight." And the nail in my coffin, "You look so pretty." I had never been the pretty girl. And now I was. I was winning. I don't know what the battle was. I have no idea what competition I had entered. But I was winning.

The only negative comment I received was from my boyfriend who told me, "You're disgusting. I can see all your bones. It's not cute." This made me angry. He's the one who started it. We'd even gotten into a body fat competition. He'd bought an electronic body fat monitor. At first, he had me beat. I was 21% body fat. My body was happy at the number. The last number I saw on that monitor was 8%. That's below the essential fat needed for a woman's body to properly function.

One of the effects of starving myself was severe mood swings. I almost always felt angry, and sometimes I would lash out. It was usually at a restaurant. I remember sitting at more than one table and crying into my plate of food. It smelled so good, and I was so hungry. But there was no way I could eat that. I ate the vegetables on my plate and played with the rest of it. The anger was replaced by a deep, overwhelming sadness.

I wanted to die. Some days I wouldn't get out of bed. Some days I would think of all the different ways I could kill myself. I wrote several suicide letters on my bedroom floor. They were all tear stained. I regularly stared at the blades of kitchen knives. I thought the cold blade would feel so good. Maybe it would warm me. Once, I put a razor to my wrist. My roommate found me before I did severe damage. I sat on the bathroom floor with her and howled. I made a pact with myself that day, and set it to expire on November 11, 2011 (11, my auspicious number). That would be the day. I would either celebrate that day, or I would end my life.

For a time, I entered into recovery, but it didn't last long. When my engagement to my boyfriend/gym partner ended, I felt my life crumble around me, so I packed my bags and moved half the world away to Turkey. Two years into my teaching stint-Turkish adventure, and just as I was rediscovering myself and joy, my period finally returned. I hadn't had a period in six years, the length of my eating disorder. I knew what this meant: my body was finally at a healthy weight again.

Despite various troubles in Turkey, I mostly kept my shit together. I had moments, but I wasn't spiraling out of control. I met a man. I fell in love. Paul was exactly what I needed, when I needed it. He celebrated me in a way that no person had ever celebrated me. I reveled in that love. I felt amazing. And, as the autumn of 2011 approached, I began to reflect on the promise I had made myself some years earlier, November 11, 2011. My day. And it became clear.

On 11-11-11, Paul and I stood on a snowy ledge atop the Grand Canyon, and I looked across that vast expanse for the first time. We collected sand, pine cones, and juniper berries and placed them in a jar, symbolically uniting ourselves. Apart from the officiant, we were alone as we said our vows there in that quiet, cold place that seemed to stretch on forever. He didn't know then what that day symbolized to me. Instead of death, I was reborn, there atop something big and wide.

I wish I could say that was the end of my struggle. Two days after we got married, we were on a plane to Saudi Arabia. It's a pretty terrible honeymoon destination, in case you were wondering. But Paul had just gotten a new job, so we were set to make the Kingdom our home. It turned out that I wasn't able to deal with the gender inequalities there. Since I'm also not really big on crimes against humanity, the experience in that place broke me.

After six months, we got out. We moved to Dubai. But it was too late. The damage was done. I needed to control something. I relapsed again, entirely in secret. For a year, I punished myself daily. Sometimes I restricted, sometimes I purged. I started drinking heavily to numb my thoughts. I threw myself into the spiral again. It felt like drowning.

Three years have passed since then, and I have done a shit ton of self-work. I've met people who made me feel safe enough to talk about my struggle. Acknowledging that I have a problem has helped me heal and move forward. I say 'have' and not 'had' because this is not something that just miraculously goes away. It's always going to be a part of me. There are always going to be triggers. I know what mine are, so I keep them out of my life. I surround myself with men and women who support each other and model self-love for me. I am no longer in a competition with myself.

Every morning I wake up, I get to make a very important choice. I get to choose either to celebrate myself or to punish myself. I get to choose love or fear. I get to choose.

And I would be lying if I said the choice is easy. Some days it is a fucking struggle. Some days I really need to control something. And some days are so rare and beautiful that the thought of how many calories are in that glass of wine or that piece of cheese doesn't even cross my mind. Some days the obsession drowns in a pool of bliss; I rejoice and cherish those days, knowing all the while that tomorrow might be different. But all I have is now. By rooting myself in the present, I'm letting go of the shame of my past and the fear of tomorrow's unknowns.

I am not alone. My experience is only a small part of a much larger collective of women (our sisters and mothers and daughters and friends), young and old, who have fed themselves off the perversions of media and a broken society. I am not alone. We are not alone. When we start a dialogue about mental health, self-harm and addiction, we can start to heal ourselves and each other. The more I allow myself to be vulnerable enough to have a discussion, to voice my constant fear that I might relapse again, the more the crushing shame lifts away.

I don't have to be embarrassed. I don't have to feel alone. But I do have to be honest. I do have to ask for help when I need it. And here, in this desert, where life seems to flourish against all odds, moments like this and communities like this give me such hope. I don't have to carry this alone.

## (FST!) Kate Ferenczi
## "A Word of Advice" January 2015

Typically, the first question I get when someone gets my clothes off is "So, are you a Taurus or are you a big Longhorns fan?" One would think, that when I'm finally naked, they'd say something else, like comment about something or tell me what they're going to do to me next, but, since I got that tattoo, those are the reactions that I get more often than not, bar none. But the answer to that question isn't quite as simple as it would seem.

I got the tattoo for free, actually. I won it at a charity raffle. I had decided I'd wanted this particular tattoo after a wild night, but didn't know when I was going to get it. I saw it as a beautiful piece of kismet in my life when I'd won.

I had to go in several times prior to getting the tattoo to speak with the artist about what I wanted done and to ensure it was within the price range of the certificate. He knew I wanted a bull. I showed him the particular one that I wanted. He also knew the size and that I wanted it all black except for some small red accents. There's just one question he didn't ask and was mighty surprised at the answer when I finally went in to get it.

"Have a seat" he said, pointing at the chair.

"Well, that wouldn't work for where I want it. Perhaps if I lie down?"

"Where do you want it?"

"My left cheek" I said smiling.

This burly, biker tattoo artist who had tattoos all the way up to the top of his head immediately looked at the cheek on my face, then at my seemingly benign school-marm outfit of a long brown skirt and a black ruffled blouse, and brought his gaze down even farther, before

187

slowly laying the chair down for me to lie upon.

Now, the story of my tattoo has nothing to do with a zodiac sign or a college football team. It has to do with an experience that I had that changed my life forever. Yes, it was in a bar. Yes, it was in Vegas. Yes, it was after a wedding. The wedding of my ex-girlfriend, actually. Yes, drinking was involved and perhaps some name calling, some bets, and some friendly banter. And of course… the bull.

But, I get ahead of myself.

It all really started when I was younger. I was a repressed child who tried so very hard to be perfect. If I was perfect, I'd have friends. If I was perfect, my mother would love me. If I was perfect, my brother would stop abusing me. If I was perfect, my teachers would adore me. If only I could be perfect. So I aimed directly for the status quo. I tried to fit in and do just as everyone else did. I dressed like them. I talked like them. I played like them. I tried to hide me as deeply as I could because I was not perfect.

My rebellious years really hit hard. By that time, my perfection was applied there. I was adept at hanging out with the reprobates and delinquents while still looking like a typical kid. I hung out with the stoners but didn't get high. I took the blow-off classes as well as the AP classes and nearly always had good grades. I strove for perfection at bucking the system, though I still lived in fear of not being accepted. A fear of not being good enough.

I continued to follow the prescription that society had laid out. It's how one becomes an adult, and does it perfectly, right? Graduate high school, go to college, get a degree, marry, have a kid. That sort of thing is just what you do, right? I strove to do those steps perfectly, too.

Then it blew up in my face. The husband walked out on me and the infant. The degree didn't give me a sustainable career. My mother still didn't accept me. The only friends I had were the ones who accepted me when I was out of the norm. I felt stifled. I was suffocating. I was dying.

188

Then, I was given the best advice ever: "Feel the fear and do it anyway."

Know the fear is there, step right into that cloud of paralyzing horror, and do what feels right anyway.

I started to take a few steps into the fear and found that once I got past that first barrier, the fear was like the curtain around the Wizard of Oz. Once you're past it, you have enough chutzpah to really keep going because it's not scary anymore.

I began to feel life really open for me. I started to see opportunities at every turn. I felt the magic of life pulse through me and I felt the love and acceptance come pouring in.

Yes, there were (and still are) a few naysayers. Typically once I'm in the midst of doing something that I love and I'm past that barrier of fear, I don't really give a fig for others' perceptions of me.

It is one of the most exhilarating feelings in the universe. Living a life free of fear.

So, there I was. Gilly's BBQ inside Treasure Island on the Las Vegas strip. Sidled up at the bar with a rum and Coke in hand, standing elbow to elbow with my newly wedded, 6 foot tall Amazon of an ex-girlfriend, Ginger. We were watching these cute little co-eds on the mechanical bull. They were all giggly and adorable, getting thrown this way and that by the guy operating the joystick attached to the leather and metal monstrosity. We began ragging on these women. These vapid twats who could hold their liquor as well as they could hold the bull, which is to say, not very well.

Then the fear came creeping in. I was too old to go up there. I am way too fat to get up on that damn thing. I'd look like a total idiot. I'd get up on there, think I was holding on, then with the first flash, I'd be thrown across the room with a concussion or a bleeding head trauma. It was best to just stay at the bar and talk shit. It's so much safer there.

Then I realized I was letting the fear drive me. I wasn't taking control. I started the easiest way possible into that fear: get someone else to come with me.

Tapping Ginger, I said "I got $20 says you and I can do better than those girls up there."

She was still living in the fear. She blew me off. Okay, I can up the ante on this one.

"Y'know, when we dated, it was back in the 90's. There's not much I remember from that decade, but the one thing I really don't remember was the part where you were a total pussy..." I stepped past my fear, looked her straight in the eye and put out my hand for her to walk through that fear with me.

Her eyes flashed. Her scowl started. She snarled as she grabbed the cash from my hand and stomped toward the bull operator.

Each of us took a turn hoisting the other's fat, awkward ass on that bull. Each of us rode the hell out of that damn thing. Ginger even broke a nail! The operator took forever to finally be able to throw either one of us off that damn thing. We grabbed life by the horns that day. We rode that shit off into the fucking sunset.

To this day, I still remember that moment—when I felt the fear and did it anyway. I even dragged a good friend along with me.

So, always remember, when you have the opportunity, grab life by the horns. Grab it and ride the hell out of it. This is the only life like this that you get. Fuck that fear and do it anyway!

## "Next Chapter" January 2014

I found my husband quivering, naked, in the empty upstairs bathtub of his Austin condo. He was holding his knees to his hairy chest. It smelled like he had thrown up.

"Angie!" he moaned, lowly, almost inaudibly. He had a gravely baritone voice; he grew up in Fort Worth singing in Baptist church choirs. He had fallen away sometime in his late teens.

"What? I'm right here." I was irritated. Hung over. We had fought the previous night in the bar, as usual, yelling over the music. But we had sex when we got back to his place, also as usual. Now why the hell was he sitting in the empty tub at two in the afternoon? Asshole.

He reached out of the bath, snatching at my arms like a desperate giant infant wanting to be lifted up. I thought he had the flu. I hadn't seen him sick in at least four years, when he was just starting his master's in Las Cruces, and I was still living in Tucson, finishing the last semester of my undergrad degree. He had some kind of super immunity.

He began to sort of claw his way out of the tub, trying to stand up, using me for support because he couldn't gain a foothold. "I've got you, I've got you, slow down." I was stressing out now. My mama/wifey instincts kicked in. I didn't have him. He is 6'1, totally built, and I'm ... smaller.

He's got that sexpot drawl. He's a half Greek, part Cherokee, dark-complected, rockabilly cowboy. Hot. When he had a bad haircut and those tacky sideburns were in style, he looked significantly like Mister Spock, but generally, he was fucking gorgeous. At that moment, though, he absolutely was not. He was not present in his body. He was pale, and scaring the hell out of me. I loved him, after all, though our fighting was so out of hand that it was better that we lived in different cities. We had been together for about six-and-a-half years. Our sex was like shooting stars, but we weren't real fond of one another a lot of the time.

Then his knees buckled and he crumpled over the tub onto the bathroom floor like he had no bones. The dog stuck her nose in, worried about her dad. I went out into the bedroom to get one of our phones to call 911.

"Wait."

"No! I'm going to …"

"I don't need an ambulance. Angie. I have to tell you something," he stammered. "I have to say it now." I remember there was no emphasis on the "now"—he made the statement with flat resignation.

My turn to collapse, that son of a bitch.

In Austin that afternoon, it was hot. No, cold. Rainy? Snowy. Does it snow in Austin? I remember standing on his condo's joke of a front porch having put a leash on the dog. Taking the dog for a walk through his ugly gated community in Barton Creek. That walk was shock made manifest. It was my response to the news, news that has shaped me more than anything anyone has ever told me before or since.

The comprehension wasn't firm or immediate. It was like when you first take acid and it starts to hit. Little chem trails, you know? Wisps of dew, blue-violet swirling. Watching the Challenger explode on the TV in your school auditorium assembly. Learning that the Towers were going down, and watching the footage over and over and over again, but knowing no one in New York.

I did some foggy math on that walk. We had met the month before I turned 21, in July 1998. He had started paying for sex in 1991. And he never even took a week off.

Time passes, not much. Driving with him and his mother to Planned Parenthood to see if I have HIV. I'm petrified of needles, so I make him take me to the only clinic in Austin that does the cheek swab test.

This is the errand that trumps all other errands: find out if it's fatal news. He had shared needles with prostitutes and certainly didn't use many condoms. He would put his wedding ring in the center console of his truck when he went into their apartment or massage parlors or horse stalls in Nogales or Juárez.

He has to pull over on the highway to the clinic because he's shaking so hard, he can't drive. He has a good heart. His mother takes over the few remaining miles. Not sure which is worse. I don't remember when she drove up from Houston. But she had, and she stayed in Austin for six months, sleeping with her son on a pullout sofa in his room. Monitoring him, she said.

Back then, the nurse had to fill out a detailed form when a patient got an HIV test.

"Reason for taking test?" she asked.

"Husband fucked hundreds of prostitutes."

The nurse looked at me and looked back down, real fast. I go out to sit in the waiting room. He waits, still shaking, looking at his feet. His mother plays a mindless game on her flip phone. I'm so alone.

The test comes out negative, which is, you know, good. I actually came out of this with zero STDs. My sister once said I have a pussy of steel.

Another scene, still in Austin. A day later or maybe earlier than the clinic visit. I had to go back to L.A. soon. I was in my first quarter at UCLA, starting my doctorate.

Me, yelling: "Where in this house did you not fuck a prostitute? Where can I sleep where you didn't come all over some ho? The couch?"

"No."

"The bed? The floor?"

"No."

"Get me a hotel."

"Ok."

I was going to "Tammy Wynette" it. I was going to stand by my man. My husband was very, very sick. He did not want to be a sex addict, of course. He wanted his sanity back, and he wanted his marriage, his health, and he was so desperately ashamed. Like heroin, getting the next fix was all he could think about since he was 17. He was then 32.

We saw his psychiatrist that week, the man who had told him that it was time to tell his wife. Together, we learned what it was going to take for him to get better. His addiction was truly severe. Porn was always there, but by then he needed a human to facilitate his orgasms, or he would not be satisfied. By then, porn was like a smoker only scrounging up half a menthol, the doctor explained, or drinking a wine cooler when your venom of choice is house whiskey, neat.

My husband said he needed me. He asked me to please consider staying with him as he found an elusive non-Christian rehabilitation clinic. He had spent his inheritance, more than a million dollars already, and was about to borrow money to go deeper into this addiction. So he had hit rock bottom.

Los Angeles, six months later.

Our rehab center was next door to Dr. Phil's office on Robertson, across from an expensive Parisian patisserie where the guys were allowed to get coffee and bear claws, supervised, once a day for 15 minutes.

It turned out to be a great gift that the $40,000 outpatient center rehabilitated not only the addict, but the spouse. Well, not really "rehabilitated the spouse" in a negative connotation sort of way, but built us spouses back up from deconstructed, weightless shells to fragile tangible things that could at least sit in chairs. Spouses went weekly, on Saturdays, never ever having contact with the addicts. This was a six-week class, during which we learned the nature of addiction, then sex addiction specifically. We prepared for what is called "disclosure."

The men, too, were preparing for disclosure.

Disclosure is when we would learn what really happened during the course of our relationships. All of it. Where our money went, what our guys were sticking their dicks into. Open mouths of young men in holey T-shirts, and glory holes in the bathroom walls of sex shops near airports. It's almost always those places you see near airports, in case you wondered. You can buy anything in those.

By the time I had the honor of learning every little thing that he had done, it was the summer between my first and second years at UCLA. That first year I had turned in gibberish instead of competent analyses of Marxist theory. I had had panic attacks in public. But thanks to that rehab center, I learned a neat concept called "personal boundaries." I decided that if he acted out again—which in his case meant used porn, went to a bar alone, or, god forbid had sex or used drugs outside of our marriage—I would file. Or technically, I'd make him file, because I certainly wasn't paying any legal fees.

He went home to Austin to sell the condo. But in October, when he called me on the phone to tell me that he had fucked a 16-year-old Hooters busgirl, I fell onto the base of the big tree outside my building at UCLA where I was standing. The tree was covered in fire ants, come to find out.

I hung up the phone. I had my answer. Probably not much in the way of sanity, but an answer. I went to the third floor bathroom, and peeled off all my clothes right in the middle of the room, starting with my flip flops and my jeans. Ants just everywhere.

Why was I never good enough? Even though he had told me during disclosure that he had paid for sex with women as young as my sister and as old as my mother, and Russian sex slaves held in Tijuana against their will, young skinny boys in vinyl on the streets of Houston, and high-priced prostitutes in what was once our bed here in Tucson, I felt insecure. I stood naked in the grey marble bathroom, just flicking ants onto the floor as they bit me. None of my students or professors walked in, thank God. I just might have died.

Numb and bitten, I walked to the parking garage, past the regal brick archaeology museum. I got in my car and drove four hours straight to Yosemite for some reason, and checked in to a bed and breakfast with a wine bar to drink myself lucid. I got in my Hyundai Accent—the only thing I got out of the divorce except a .357 Magnum and some Mexican furniture that we had commissioned near Juárez. A Hyundai and a handgun. Now I know what he was doing in Mexico while I was working with those furniture craftsmen. Now I know why it took so long for him to go get lunch on our honeymoon in Peru. Now I know.

What I don't know is where he is now. What I don't know is if he is doing this to other women. I don't know if he's HIV positive. The chances are 50-50. I'd like to believe he sequestered himself in a cabin in the woods to protect the world from his broken self. That would be in his nature too. He has a good heart.

As for me, it's been 10 years since we spoke, since the divorce was finalized. I do forgive him. He makes for a great story. That chapter has been closed for quite some time. I don't want protection, I don't want sympathy, and I don't want to be taken care of. I have a pussy of steel.

## "Luck Be a Lady" March 2016

I started taking the pill when I was nineteen years old. My sex life was still shiny and new, but I was in a hurry to break it in, and at nineteen, I had my very first pregnancy scare.

For days I prayed to a god I didn't believe in, went mountain biking on the roughest trails, and checked my underwear like a winning lottery ticket was about to fall out of me. I'm pretty sure the mountain biking and the stress were what caused my urinary tract infection, and when the nurse took my pee and I asked what they were going to test it for, she knew what I meant. When she told me I didn't have a kidney infection or a fetus, it was like that part in the Wizard of Oz where it goes from black and white to color. Everything looked normal again.

It was the summer after my freshman year of college, and I was working at a mountain resort three hours' drive from school. The daddy candidate had gone back to the girlfriend he'd dumped for me. I called him from the pay phone in the parking lot of the hotel and told him I'd thought I was pregnant, but I wasn't, and thanks a lot for nothing and I hate you. I was so relieved and my relief made me tell the truth.

For most of my twenties, I got my pills from Planned Parenthood. It was affordable and discreet; in other words, I probably wouldn't be running into my mom there.

My first visit, I sat in the waiting room and tried not to look at the girls and women around me and wonder who might be getting an abortion that day. After I'd endured the exam and the questions and was finally able to walk out of there with that cool plastic clamshell case and three months' worth of freedom from fear, I stopped thinking about those girls and women. They'd been unlucky. That wasn't going to be me.

I was a terrible pill-taker. I was good at first – never missing one, always taking them at the same time of day, and making sure I knew when I was on the third pack so I could re-fill before running out. That maybe lasted a year. The pill is good at lulling you into complacency, and convincing you that you're not getting pregnant because you're just awesomely infertile or because your boyfriend smokes so much pot. Maybe it seems improbable because the pill is so small. How could something that tiny stop the UNSTOPPABLE FORCE OF LIFE? That my boyfriend's sperm were half-lidded stoners who fell asleep before they could get to my egg was far more plausible. No pregnancy scares and his broody eyes and droll wit made him husband material.

Five weeks after we got married, we moved to Tokyo so I could pursue my dream of teaching English in windowless cubicles to housewives and exhausted teenagers. Planned Parenthood let me buy a year's worth of pills because I had no idea how Japanese people did these things. The pill turned out to be just as much of a pain to get in Japan. Probably more so, since I didn't speak Japanese. The one time I did go to a hospital there, nobody spoke English and there's only so far you can get with gestures. My amateur sign-language for "birth control" would have looked a lot like I was trying to get a prescription for cyanide. [Mimes popping pill, pointing at uterus, and universal symbol for choking].

When the pills and my tolerance for Tokyo ran out, we moved back to the U.S. so I could go to grad school. That's when we stopped having sex. Not like cold turkey, but for folks who'd only been married a little over a year, it was at least lukewarm turkey. I kept taking the pill for a while, and then I let the last pack run out. I told myself and him it was because I was in school, and didn't make enough money to justify it and we could just use condoms but neither of us liked them, so the times we did do it, we relied on his impeccable sense of timing.

But I was scared every time, and every month I waited for my period like a tax return. My fear followed us to Bosnia, where I got my first real job teaching English in a university. One month, I was so terrified I was pregnant that I sat on our toilet crying for fifteen minutes until Gabe went out and bought a pregnancy test. When he came back he told me they sold oral contraceptives over the counter. The test was negative, and the world went back to color.

I didn't buy the pills, though. Partly, I was convinced they had a bad effect on me—I felt irritated, prone to outbursts mostly directed at Gabe, and fatter. I didn't like that the onus was on me to make sure we didn't have a kid. I kind of felt like I was doing the lion's share of everything else adult-related in our life and was pissed that this, too, was my responsibility and my burden.

I hear how this sounds, and I know that some guys might say that condoms are a concession the guy makes. I'm gonna abandon all diplomacy here because this is FST! and say NO THEY FUCKING AREN'T. Condoms are not something you have to remember to take every goddamn morning (or evening or shit! I gotta take two this morning), or endure scrutiny of your nethers and your intentions and your purity for; they are not something you have to remember to get a prescription for, and if you forget that prescription because you are human and therefore flawed, you do not have to wait for your doctor to call it in to the pharmacy for you, maybe in the next couple weeks if you're lucky. Condoms are not a concession—they are a by-product of the luck of being born male-bodied and therefore free to decide when and whether you're going to make life. Women are not so lucky; at least, weirdly, American women.

In three of the four foreign places where I've lived—Bosnia, Ethiopia, and Southeast Asia—oral contraceptives are sold like candy or soda, over the counter and without a prescription. In these places my parents were reluctant to visit, where clean water was hard to come by and I feared food poisoning and malaria, I could freely buy a pill that would alleviate my fear of pregnancy. I could (and did) walk into a pharmacy in Bangkok and walk out with an armload of little pink boxes.

As luck would have it, I have somehow managed to evade the miracle of life, even with my shoddy track record and questionably principled stands. There have been close calls, the closest of which was when I started an affair with a man in Burma, while Gabe was still in the States. If there's a god up there who smites women the way some folks say he does, he must have fallen asleep at the switch with my name on it.

The last time I stopped taking the pill was last October. It was the evening before I was to leave on a long weekend trip with Steve (aka, man in Burma, now husband), and I'd been writing "BC" (for birth control) on my hand all week to remember to re-fill my prescription. At the Safeway pharmacy, they told me my prescription had expired, and my doctor had to call in a new one. No check-up required—just a call from a doctor, whose approval I had already received to block a baby, and apparently needed to receive again, one arbitrary year later. The pointlessness of this overwhelmed me, and I raged through the store, shouting to no one in particular, "I can get a gun that would kill a kid easier than I can get a pill that will prevent one from being born!"

Afterward, on the way to New Mexico, Steve says he'll get a vasectomy. I am grateful, but it's a messy gratitude. I feel a principled stand creeping in. His choices come so easily, and even surgery is no big deal; it's done in the doctor's office in a couple minutes. We could go out to dinner after.

I read recently they're developing a sperm switch. No kidding, the headline read: "Men can turn fertility on and off with new invention." Ladies: we have our luck and we have our choices that we fight tooth and nail for, that we are judged for, that we jump through hoops for, and meanwhile, science devotes itself to making the male contraceptive version of The Clapper.

My heretofore unfertilized eggs may indeed be the result of more than a little luck, but the most miraculous thing, I think, the luckiest thing, is that women's rage has not spilled over, that we don't weep every day at this blatant imbalance and injustice, and, as Joan Holloway would say, that we don't burn this place to the ground.

**FST!** Amy Robertson
## "Fish Out of Water" April 2016

In middle school, I developed a crippling fear of speaking in a foreign language. Come to think of it, Middle School is where I developed pretty much all of my social anxieties. Looking back at my 7th grade Spanish class, I've realized that my peers dispensed their ridicule indiscriminately. But at the time, to my little middle school, insecure brain, it sure felt personal. In total, I slogged through NINE years of Spanish (nine years!).

And at the end of it all, I could say five things.

Five things.

That's not even a thing per year!

It didn't help that later, when I thought Spanish was out of my life for good, my college boyfriend—who was fluent in Spanish—laughed at my pronunciation, my ignorance of conjugation, and my pathetic digression into pantomime every time I tried to speak. He said he laughed because "it was cute." But it was crippling.

These combined experiences of malicious middle schoolers and an insecure dating life, cultivated a rich, paralyzing terror deep within me.

A terror that I, unfortunately, still have.

Fast-forward a few years.

I am now dating a Polish boy. One of the many aspects that makes me absolutely twitterpated over him is that he is a dancer, like me. And, unlike many of the men I've met at social dance clubs, he clearly does it because he loves it, and not just to get laid. This aspect was made clear by his genre: Traditional Polish Folk Dancing. I'm pretty sure no one has joined a Polish folk dancing group to get laid... that is, until I joined the group.

It's been wonderful (the sex AND the dancing). Polish dance has literally taken over my life and I have become obsessed. Being in a traditional Polish folk dancing group though, it really was only a matter of time before the subject of learning to speak Polish came up.

Let me tell you a little something about Polish: it's fucking hard.

It is utterly, and quite literally, foreign.

Let me give you a mini lesson. I thought that, for some reason, I would be able to recognize the word for "English." So one of my first Polish lessons, I was like, "Alright! Let's start with something easy! What's the word for English?"

… It's po angielsku.

Yeeeeah... Nope. Didn't recognize that word.

Luckily, my boyfriend and his family have been absolutely wonderful in encouraging me to learn, speak, and sing *cringe* in Polish. Unfortunately though, I still suffer horrendously from my insecurities. To the point where, someone will jabber at me in Polish, a simple greeting—and I'll even know how to respond—but I just can't. I freeze up, my eyes bulge and I get this terrified deer-in-the-headlights look that oftentimes makes the Polish speakers switch to English and ask if I'm okay.

"Yeah, yeah, I'm… fine" now that we're back to speaking English.

In 2014, our Polish folk dancing group, Lajkonik, was invited to perform at an International Dance Festival in Poland. My overwhelming excitement to tour and perform in Poland was only slightly overshadowed by my nervousness of navigating a foreign country. But this is where the perk of having a bilingual boyfriend comes in. Plus, several members of Lajkonik were fluent in Polish.

In fact, there were only a few of us that didn't speak Polish. This included my dear friend Julie.

So we went to Poland. And it was amazing (oh my gosh, I ate so many pierogi!).

It was a very surreal feeling, walking down the streets of these tiny towns, where no one spoke English, and being the "exotic foreigners." It was also remarkably overwhelming to never be able to understand anyone around you.

Everywhere you went, it was just a jabber jabber jabber...

So one thing happened, that I don't think either Julie or I expected, and that was this feeling of helplessness. We were almost completely dependent on the Polish-speaking members of the group to translate for us. This could lead to varying degrees of frustration; depending on if your translator was the boyfriend, or a Polish diva.

Now, Julie and I like to think of ourselves as strong, independent women who are used to handling shit by ourselves, so being in this situation was actually really uncomfortable. We couldn't just ask someone where the bathroom was, or what was for dinner. This finally came to a head in the tiny village of Opoczno.

It was there that Julie and I decided we needed to accomplish something, anything, by ourselves. So we decided on finding an ATM. It was the perfect plan. Once we got translated directions, there was absolutely no human contact needed.

In hindsight, I don't really know why we thought this was such a good idea, to just wander around an unfamiliar place where no one spoke English, but we were pretty desperate to reassert our independence.

So, we got our directions: "Down that street, past the market, by that one tree, you know the one with the berries that make that jam, next to the bank."

Cool.

We got this.

Well, found the bank, but no ATM.

"Okay, well, let's go in the bank and see if it's in there."

The difference between Polish banks and American banks is another thing I'd never really thought about. I think Julie and I both expected a large lobby, where you could stand by the door, unnoticed, get your bearings and it not be too awkward.

Well, we walked into this bank and *bam* there were just two women.

That's it.

No lobby, no place to take your bearings. There was no space there to not be awkward. There wasn't even a potted plant to hide behind.

This unexpected shock left Julie and me standing there, probably looking very startled in a very normal situation.

One of the women politely inquired something … in Polish.

And inside, I'm like: Shit shit shit shit shit.

Then I was like, No! Wait! Amy Nicole you were trained for this! You know how to ask if they understand English! Come on! Do it!

But instead, I was only able to squeak inaudibly, "po angielsku??"

Yeah, they didn't understand that.

Next plan: maybe, just maybe one of these women understood English! I mean… that would make her the only woman in the entire village that did, but it was either try that or scuttle awkwardly back out the door, so I said, "English?"

They frown, politely, "Nie." (That means no in Polish!)

"Umm… ATM?"

"Nie."

Dammit.

I looked desperately to Julie, my last line of defense before the awkward scuttle, and she desperately pantomimed the ATM experience: She typed at an imaginary keypad in the air and hummed the little jingle that accompanies each button being push. She made an elaborate electronic whirling noise demonstrating cash being dispensed and did a little victory jiggle at receiving the cash out of the air.

Overall, it was one of the most adorable things I'd ever seen. However, I was unsure of how effective it would be at communicating "ATM."

I glanced back at the bank ladies in time to see comprehension dawn on their faces, "Oh!!" they cried "Tak tak, bankomat bankomat!" and pointed us to the ATM, which was across the street. The four of us all took a moment to celebrate our successful communication with some further victory jiggles and shared giggles, then we were back on our way.

I have never been so happy after accomplishing such a mundane task.

So that day, Julie taught me a something very important. When it came to talking to people in another language, I could cheat! I could pantomime and dance to communicate. This was such a relief; I wasn't completely helpless if I got stranded. I might look a little silly gesturing everything out, but I could communicate with the people around me! Just knowing that allowed me to relax substantially. Julie had thrown me a life raft.

And now, after two and a half years, with my pantomime life raft and my boyfriend's unending patience, I have officially broken my foreign language record of five things in Spanish: in Polish, I can say six things!

Na zdrowie! (cheers!)

I've never been what you'd call a joiner. As a kid, I much preferred to be alone, and even when my parents tried to push me toward peer camaraderie, it didn't work. I agreed to join the Girl Scouts when I was in second grade. While the other girls were interested in friendship bracelets, outdoor games, and songs, I was there to fill my sash with brightly colored little embroidered patches, and to sell cookies. Not just to sell cookies, I was there to sell the MOST cookies. After I did (it was no contest—those girls didn't know what hit 'em), I asked my mom if I really truly had to finish out the year and go on that horrid camping trip. I think she was pretty tired of me being the weird loner Brownie, so she was cool with it. I don't think she really wanted to go camping either.

In high school though, I joined two sports teams. I did one season each of swimming and bowling. I've since been told that these aren't really team sports. In both, while I technically had teammates around me, I liked that they had no effect at all on whether I picked up that spare, which I often did, or swam the fastest, which I rarely did. My success or my failure, but it was mine alone.

Since joining the workforce, I've found that in every single job interview committee is looking for someone who's a team player. "Are you a team player?" "Describe a time in your career when you were a team player." I've obviously found ways to answer this question, because I have a job, but reading between the lines here, they just want to know if you're the kind of selfish bastard who cares more about your personal success and happiness over the greater good of the company. Once, my two-person department was nominated for, and won, the Outstanding Team Award. Two months later, I left that job for more money.

So all that said, I wasn't really sure what I was going to talk about on the theme of Team Player.

Does it count that sometimes, my cat and I will compromise on our Netflix choice for the night?

But then I remembered one type of team I've enjoyed being a part of, so much so that it never felt like the socially pressured drudgery I'd always assumed was just part of a team experience: an incredibly serious, high-stakes quiz team.

I started going to Geeks who Drink after a breakup, looking for something to do with my time, and just get out of the house and have some semblance of a social life. Sitting around at a bar answering trivia questions fit the bill. I began recruiting some of my roommates and grad school friends to come with me, and started meeting people there, too. I met Ingrid and Luke one night, they were on an opposing team at the table next to mine. They were more welcoming, less cliquish and antagonistic than other teams, but still fiercely competitive and insanely knowledgeable. I met Andrew shortly after, finding ourselves on the same team one night because of a mutual friend. We hit it off after our team won first place that night, and he then asked me to shush him like a librarian.

Within the next few months, the four of us went to one or two quiz nights a week, often playing together under the moniker Drum Major Sex Panther, which Ingrid had been using for some time. It worked though, because two of the team members had been drum majors in their high school marching bands (buncha nerds) and remaining members identified as sex panthers by default. Sixty percent of the time, we got the question right every time.

And once a year, Geeks Who Drink holds a massive, national quiz event, lovingly named Geek Bowl. Ingrid had been once before, and we'd heard from our regular quizmasters that it was a stupidly fun time and we should go if we could. Geek Bowl was calling to us. On some level for a fun vacation (they held it in Austin) but also to know if we could hold our own on a larger stage, cautiously testing what drunk little know-it-alls we were.

We were going to fucking Nationals.

Now, let me tone down expectations slightly. There was no bar we had to meet in order to qualify. If you can get six people together and pay the entry fee, you're in. "Going to Nationals" probably just means that you take this whole thing too seriously, but this was about all I had going on in my life and I needed it.

Full of excitement and bravado that we hoped we could back up, we flew to Austin. The meet and greet party the night before the quiz was held in a beer garden, with live-band karaoke and a mix and mingle version of Cards Against Humanity. Upon arrival, each participant was handed a white card; all the quizmasters had black cards to match to. My card was Balls, so it already felt like a winning night.

I met the two local players that Ingrid had recruited to round out our team, James and Chelsea, whom she'd met last year at Geek Bowl. Chelsea did not fuck around, and basically knew everything and everyone surrounding the quiz scene. James was supposed to be some kind of trivia ninja, who started going to Geeks Who Drink as a one-man team until Chelsea absorbed him into her group. I can only imagine that was a direct, no-nonsense interaction. Chelsea approached me, all-business, midway through the party: "What's your deal, are you available, I have people asking about you." Wait, am I the hot girl at Geek Bowl?! This is home, and I'm never leaving. We took team photos together, hit the karaoke stage, and we had an all-around great time. We clicked. For once, it felt awesome being part of a team.

And finally the next day, the time had arrived. As we walked into the Austin Music Hall, where over 150 round tables were set up over two levels, it hit me that this was no longer a fun party. This was the main event, and we did not come all this way to fuck it up. I took notice of the fact that the line for the men's restroom was much longer than that for the women's, but both paled in comparison to the line for the bar. Better start with a double so I don't have to get back in that line anytime soon. The venue was packed with people who, well, not to stereotype, but were about what you'd expect at an event called Geek Bowl.

And hung from the balcony were banners of team support, state pride, and smack talk. As we found our table, we spotted a banner made by one of the Tucson quizmasters, painted with the Arizona state flag, a saguaro cactus, and the phrase: "Arizona: 110 Degrees of

208

Awesome."

You're damn right. We quickly learned that we were the only team representing Arizona. Maybe because of where our state tends to fall in terms of education rankings, it felt like we had something to prove, and needed to seriously represent. A bit daunted by the scale of this thing, we looked at each other around the table and revealed our hopes for the outcome. Loudly, it was "Go big or go home, top ten!" and more discreetly settling on top 25% as the point at which we'd be okay with things.

I have to take a moment to say, this massive scale trivia competition was basically heaven for the little girl who didn't want to spend time around other kids, but rather escaped into old movies and TV shows. This is a world in which guilty pleasures lose all their guilt. If we get the point, no explanation or apology needed about why you know the shitty things you know, like that you are one hundred percent confident that the artist of that song is Bowling for Soup, yes, I promise that's correct.

There's a level of trust that you build with one another over the confidence in your knowledge—are you sure you're sure?—and a real challenge when teammates are confident about different answers. There was a debate over whether or not oregano would have been a common enough household ingredient during the first publication of Joy of Cooking, or if it would have been too "ethnic" at the time. Later, our Austin teammates nearly got to fisticuffs debating what, precisely, was the title of the final book in the Fifty Shades trilogy. It's Fifty Shades Freed, in case you're wondering, and yes we got it right.

After the first three rounds (out of eight), scores were projected like scrolling credits on the giant screen which served as a stage backdrop. There were 150-odd teams, and they had to keep it at a pace that drunk people could read, so the scrolling took a while. First break, Drum Major Sex Panther was number 69 (lolz and stuff). After three more rounds, we were pleased to see we'd climbed up to 52! Not where we wanted, but we hadn't yet used the joker, which allows you to double your score on one round. I'd like to say we saved it until the end for suspense, but I think we just weren't confident enough about a round yet.

After the final round, DMSP took a collective sigh of relief. Done using my brain for the evening, I made my way to the bar for another stiff drink, while the talent show began. There were some fun performances, but the clear audience favorite, and eventual winner, was a guy who sang the Muppet Babies theme song in falsetto, complete with spot-on impressions of every character. It was awesome.

Okay, back to business. The scrolling started up again. Team names and rankings scrolled, and scrolled, and scrolled, and we still weren't listed. We cheered a bit when 52 passed, knowing that we'd improved. Top quartile? Sure, we still hadn't seen our name by the mid-30's. Wait, top ten? No way. And just before 5th place was revealed, the scrolling stopped. We looked at each other around the table, asking if we were positive they'd not shown us. Maybe we'd missed it? 5th place was revealed. Still not us. And then over the speakers: there's a tie for 3rd place.

Independence Hall and Oates and Drum Major Sex Panther to the stage for a tiebreaker round.

Oh, shit. I looked at the empty glass in front of me that had very recently held a double whiskey, neat. At regular quiz events, tiebreakers tend to be dance-offs. Not here. After we danced and cheered our way through the sea of tables, we stood on opposite ends of the stage from our Philadelphia-based opponents and were handed a dry erase board and marker, while questions loomed on the giant screen over our heads.

Ultimately, it came down to the final question of the tiebreaker round, in which we had to do math, using answers to other questions, like the number of whatevers times the quantity of the thing, plus the year this happened, divided by the age of so-and-so. Closest to the correct number won. I do not remember the question, but I do remember how poor my grasp was on order of operations, drunk and onstage in front of a thousand people.

Our answers were revealed, and Independence Hall and Oates were way off... yet we were even further. They took the 3rd place prize, a comedy-sized check for $1200, and we got the 4th place consolation: six GIANT teddy bears and a bottle of Manischewitz wine that we finished before we left the stage.

We were so exuberant that we didn't really even see who won first or second, as we paraded and celebrated past the literally hundreds of people we'd just beaten, who could have all given us the stink eye or been an ass about how badly we bombed that final question. Nobody did, though. People congratulated us and offered to take group pictures. Our fun and excitement was contagious and people celebrated with us. We weren't just acting like drunk know-it-alls, we were a group of people who'd come to have fun doing something we enjoy.

With our shocked and delighted expressions onstage, we probably looked like the underdogs, in a room full of people who had most certainly felt like an underdog at one point or another. People were talking about that Arizona team, and partied it up with us as we bar-hopped through Austin fueled by alcohol and adrenaline, with human-sized teddy bears in tow, Ingrid in her drum major hat, me wearing the Arizona state flag like a superhero cape. With the exception of FST!, that night was the most I'd ever felt like part of a community, like... well, a team. To paraphrase the motto of Pawnee, Indiana, we were first in friendship, even if we were fourth in quiz. Or third and a half, as we'll usually claim.

I'd like to tell my younger self that being a team player doesn't have to be about being the best, or sacrificing yourself, or being dependent on someone. Maybe in order to be a team player, you just need to find the right team. Maybe it's the right people, who are a perfect complement to your brand of weird. Maybe it's just about working together with those people toward your goals, doing things you really enjoy: like drinking and being right about things.

FST! Female StoryTellers present:

A LETTER to AMYONE ♥ FST! xoxo

When? MAY 31 7:00 PM

Be there →

LoveSmack STUDIOS
19 East Toole
Tucson, AZ

$7 suggested donation

FST! #2

facebook.com/FStoryTellers

Dear Cancer,

I think most people would start this letter with a "Screw You!"

That was my initial response when I first got my diagnosis. Actually, that was my third response. I didn't hit the detonation button until I got over Shock and Denial phases.

However, I did wonder, "Why me?" I think we all go through that. The more salient question for me, though, was "Why does it have to be brain cancer?"

Breast cancer is all the rage. Even the NFL wears pink in October to show their love for titties. Don't get me wrong – I love me some tatas, especially Double D's.

You can take my boobs, Cancer. I'm barely a C-cup. Take my ovaries. Take my colon. I can handle depositing my #2s in a bag. But my brain? Really? That's just rude.

I've never considered myself to be a looker. Never. I do have a nice bedonkedonk. I'm aaaaaalll about that bass.

I used to try to blend into the background when I was in junior high. I was in honors-level classes. But even amongst the geeks, I wasn't chic. And then, it happened. I discovered . . . the debate team. I was allowed to have an opinion and speak my mind. I read Time and Newsweek, instead of Glamour or Vogue. Research was a perfectly "normal" pastime.

Dear Cancer,

You tried to take my best asset away from me.

Why?

Why?

~ ~ ~ ~ ~

Dear Cancer,

I am able to acknowledge that you're not an asshole. Radiation and chemo are the true villains in this story.

~ ~ ~ ~ ~

Dear Radiation,

I didn't mind losing my hair during treatment. You're talking to a self-identified radical feminist who used to shave her head on the regular to show the patriarchy that beauty standards are some buuuuullshiiiiit.

Baldness is great for a gal on the go, such as myself. I have a sleeeew of supporters who have given me scarves, hats, and other fashion accessories to adorn my beautiful bald head.

I am not ashamed to be bald.

This bitch rolls with panache.

But you robbed me of my voice, Radiation. That's just cold.

Do you know how it feels to go from being a zinester,

turned blogger,

turned published freelancer journalist

to someone who can't remember how to send a simple email,

let alone

remember her own name?

It sucks, okay. It really sucks.


~ ~ ~ ~ ~


Dear Radiation,

I will admit that I have a love-hate relationship with you. The science behind radiation makes me tingle. It's a fine mix between Star Wars light sabers and getting beamed aboard the Starship Enterprise.

My first appointment at the radiation clinic was awkward. The lab techs had me lie down face up on the table. They made a plastic mold of my face so that they could make a cage for my head. You can't move your head during treatment because the laser beams' trajectory is so precise.

As the doors of the treatment room closed, I felt like Hannibal Lecter strapped down to a table in solitary.

The radiation team let me pick the music I wanted to listen to while hundreds of laser beams infiltrated my skull. I brought an acoustic guitar album of Christmas carols, along with my stuffed monkey, Little Jerry Seinfeld. I did my best to remain still while I felt the table move around. I prayed to the Sacred Elements and asked my grandfather's spirit to hold my hand. I counted the clicks of the radiation machine and timed the intervals of the different colored rays as they emanated in the tube. I experienced seizures during several treatments because of my anxiety. The techs opened the door and waited with me until I knew who I was, then repositioned me on the table so we could start from the beginning.

Family and friends took turns driving me to treatment and waiting for me in the lobby. I was served an extra-large helping of humility every day for six weeks.

I took this as an opportunity to wear a different hat or headscarf to each appointment. I told you. I'm fierce. And anyway, when the S-dawg gets prezzies from her peeps, it's a good thing.

By the end of the regimen, I earned the right to ring the bell they kept outside the treatment area.

So thank you, Radiation, for all the fabulous fashion accessories.


~ ~ ~ ~ ~


Dear Chemotherapy,

I am so over you. I'm done sitting at home all day because I am exhausted. I'm tired of eating fast food because I don't have the energy to cook dinner. I'm finished vacillating between constipation and diarrhea. And I'm fed up with getting hooked up to an IV pole every other week. I'm not going to schedule my life around toxic injections.

I am not the kind of woman who puts up with anyone's bullshit. I chose my own name for a reason. I don't belong to anyone. And I definitely don't belong to you.

Guess what? The fist-raising feminist is not going to wallow in a cesspool of self-pity. I'm going to keep taking names and kicking ass. I've busted my hump to revive my voice. My brain might resemble Swiss cheese, but my neuro-transmitters have bulked up. My brain is like Chyna from the WWF, may she rest in peace.

Dear Cancer,

I want to thank you for helping me prioritize my life. I used to be overly cautious about sharing my feelings because I didn't want to be labeled as "weak." I give hugs now. I tell my friends and family that I love them. It may be the last time we see each other in this life.

I am the grateful for learning what love really means. It's disappointing to me that many cancer survivors have partners who cut ties with them when life gets complicated.

I am truly blessed to have a partner who has put up with all kinds of shenanigans. He's eaten more than his fair share of Eegee's because I've been too tired to make dinner, let alone do the dishes. He's held my hand during green coffee enemas, and he has never made fun of me when I've pooped my pants. Shannon has listened to me repeat myself like a broken record because I can't remember what I've just said. He has read chapters of Harry Potter out loud to help me get to sleep. He even dropped out of grad school to work at a call center so that we would have stable income and health care insurance. If that isn't love, I don't know what is.

You have humbled me, Cancer, and helped me realize that it's okay to accept help from other people. I don't have to go it alone.

Humility itself is a sign of strength because it means that I recognize that I still have a lot to learn in this life, and so much more to accomplish.

Thank you for helping me acknowledge that everyone is terminal. My expiration date isn't up yet. But just in case it is, at least I won't leave this Life with any regrets. Just love. And for that, I thank you.

Sincerely,
Serena Freewomyn
Four-year Warrior

FST! presents:

SHAMELESS

August 22, 2013

7:30 PM
Doors open at 7pm

@ Beowulf
Alley Theatre
11 S 6th Ave. Tucson
*ASL Interpreters provided.

$7 Suggested
Donation
(cash only)

Partial proceeds will benefit

BODY LOVE
A WOMEN'S CONFERENCE
CHANGE YOUR WORLD, NOT YOUR BODY
"an event to promote positive body
images and confidence for women"
BodyLoveConference.com

FST! Female
StoryTellers
Facebook.com/FStoryTellers

# Best of FST! Contributors

FST! **Amanda Barth** is a fan of variety—and consequently a "Jane of All Trades"—who is inspired by life, love, and landscape. She is a teacher, a traveler, an artist, an actor, a dancer, a martial artist, a gourmand, a linguaphile, and above all else, a passionate scientist. Amanda is motivated to seek reverence, justice and equality for all Earthlings, and she can find the humor in practically anything.

FST! **Sari Beliak** is a writer and comedian. She is a contributor to ClickHole, Reductress, Runt of the Web, and the Hard Times where she gets paid to write about Morrissey. She lives in Phoenix with her dog Johnny Marr.

FST! **Cat Belue** believes that words have the power to heal and that we can all find common humanity through our stories. She also thinks her air freshener is her uncle Herbie, a space alien, so keep that in mind.

FST! **Tiara Bertram** is a 22-year-old aspiring Zumba instructor with a degree in Sociology and a passion for Subway sandwiches. Her main hobbies are reading, eating Nutella, and Netflixing for hours at a time. She enjoys writing, but her blog is currently inactive, so instead you can follow her on Twitter (@tiarafying). She believes that words hold the power of creation and is learning to speak into existence the life that she wants. She now lives in Boston, trying to figure out what she wants to do for a career.

FST! **Mel Blumenthal** is proud to be on the executive board of FST! and is working to launch pilot programs to bring storytelling into public schools to empower the next generation of tellers of tales. She is a retired professional ballroom dancer who still enjoys a good milonga and loves to salsa and bachata until unreasonable hours of the evening. She is the Vice President of the Advocacy Council for the Department of Gender and Women's Studies at the University of Arizona. The other cape she wears during the day is as a retirement consultant and finance educator, specializing in financial planning for women. She is honored to be a part of the FSTerhood!

A self-proclaimed loner who accidentally helped build a community, **(FST!) Stephanie Carlson** agreed to perform in the very first FST! show as a personal challenge to conquer her fears, and has since been onstage for a dozen shows and behind the scenes for dozens more. She's incredibly fond of craft beer, classic film, and drag queens, all of which have a wonderful home in Tucson. She moonlights as a part-time podcaster on Smitten With Smut and social media manager for her one-eyed cat, Sparrow.

**(FST!) Annie Conway** has been living, working in, and loving Tucson for over a decade. She maintains she is not an animal person, but her current animal count is ten chickens, two tortoises, and one cat. She tries to travel as much as possible and is regularly grateful for the breaks her current job in the public school system affords her.

**(FST!)Bethany Evans** is a storyteller and comedian. She performs regularly with FST! Female StoryTellers, and has been on its executive board since 2013. She has opened for Myq Kaplan, and has performed stand-up at Laffs Comedy Caffe, Tucson Improv Movement, Romo Tonight Live, Tucson Comedy Arts Festival, Laughing Liberally, Comedy at the Wench, and The Switch Comedy. She also produces and hosts The Dating Game, and was a guest on the SideStreets Podcast, Thank You for Being a Podcast, and Smitten With Smut. In her spare time, Bethany enjoys writing Game of Thrones fan fiction and teaching herself to yodel.

**(FST!) Kate Jack Ferenczi** has taken the stage seven times since their first storytelling in May, 2014 and has hosted once. They have been a professional clown, slung tea on stage, gotten a hug from a president, been dry humped by an all-male burlesque troupe, enchanted a biker gang with their mad karaoke skills, and survived eating pop-rocks while drinking a Coke. Kate Jack has also had a career as a university professor, a sign language interpreter, and now plays with stickers and colored pencils in the darkest recesses of a CPA office.

(FST!) **Amber Frame** is a writer, painter, stand-up comedian, storyteller, and part-time carny. Born in Tucson but raised on the east coast, she returned to her homeland in 2014 in search of some desert magic. She found it—in friendships, travel, comedy, family, love, cacti, and of course, FST! This book marks her first publication.

(FST!) **Serena Freewomyn** loves writing, quilting, and raising her feminist fist to call out the patriarchy. Serena claimed the feminist label when she was in high school, when Hillary Clinton told the UN Human Rights commission that "women's rights are human rights." Serena is currently working on a historical novel about Susan B. Anthony and Elizabeth Cady Stanton. Her goal is to help young women recognize that they are strong, smart, and independent; that they can be anything they want to be; and that being a grrrl is the best thing they can do.

(FST!) **Maryann Green** is an actor, director, writer and producer of theatre, and has performed with Female Storytellers since 2013. She is the Executive Director of the Tucson Fringe Festival. She spends her days molding the hearts and minds of tomorrow by teaching high school and the best compliment she's ever gotten on her writing or storytelling is "Ouch. That hits a little too close to home."

(FST!) **Benjamin Z. Griffith** is a transplant Tucson native of nearly 25 years, having moved from Harrisburg, PA, when he was 8 years old. He recently graduated from The University of Arizona with a Bachelor's of Arts in Creative Writing. Benjamin strives to be there for the community in any way he can, always putting his heart into his work. He has been involved in activism involving LGBTQ rights/issues and has volunteered with several organizations in the LGBTQ community in Tucson for several years. He enjoys art and music (especially singing), introspective discussions, and chilling with his cat, Tumbleweed.

[FST!] **Athena Hagen-Krause** is a multidisciplinary artfag, teaching artist, and craftsperson based in Tucson, Arizona. Hagen has worked within the realm of professional stagecraft, theatre education, and alternative/street theatre from a very early age. Her current focus is on the development of various workshops which use simple, creative means to explore themes of consent and body sovereignty, grief, and personal and societal transformation.

[FST!] **Nöel Hennessey** spends her days at the University of Arizona College of Engineering Academic Affairs Office, and her nights in the UA College of Education Educational Policy Studies and Practice department. In her free time, she chronicles the life of her dog, Levi, on Instagram (#levijenkins), writes for FST!, co-hosts a podcast called Smitten with Smut, rock climbs and runs marathons with her current husband, who is wonderful. She wants anyone who has survived domestic violence to know they are not alone.

Educator, kitchen witch, dog mom, and aspiring professional adventurer. In her free time, [FST!]**Jamie** can be found sunning herself on rocks, planning her next Halloween costume, or relaxing in nature with a bottle of wine.

[FST!] **Erin Jaye** is a desert-dwelling multilingual nerd of words. Activist. Chingona.

[FST!] **Kate Kincaid** is a queer, witchy, spiritual seeker, activist, and educator. She and her two partners and their partners and their partner's partners are a part of a growing community of likeminded folks. Her fascination with relationships and sexuality lead her to pursue a fulfilling career as a mental health therapist. She owns a small private practice specializing in counseling people in alternative relationship models (non-monogamy/polyamory). Her personal and professional beliefs are informed by feminism and social justice, seeing much of the dis-ease in our lives is rooted in a normal response to a broken system that is then pathologized and stigmatized.

FST! **D. Larson** has lived in Tucson for almost two decades, making her practically a native. She moved to the city for college and never left. She loves the desert, cats, music, and writing stories.

FST! **Melanie Madden** is a writer from Barstow, California, whose work has appeared in Timber Journal, The Mojave River Review, and The Feminist Wire. She holds an MFA in Creative Nonfiction from the University of Arizona and sits on the executive board of FST! Female Storytellers.

Raised in Prescott, Arizona, FST! **Angela Orlando** is a mountain girl who thrives on studying people, writing about them, and teaching college students about different ways of being human. She is all better now.

As child of the border, FST! **Susana Perez-Abreu's** life has been defined by the "in between" of being bicultural, bilingual, bimodal, and bilateral. She's a fervent Gemini, teacher, therapist, mother, wife, and sister. She is defined by her various roles and yet not at all. Her passion for storytelling came as she sought to process the most troublesome aspects of her life. Out of this adventure came a woman who found herself amidst the inbetween of the good and the bad. She has come to understand that storytelling is in her blood as it has been for her ancestors and all the chingonas that have come before her.

FST! **Alexx Ramirez** loves to tell stories, mostly about how hedgehogs, coffee, pending legislation, and comics on TheOatmeal.com affect her daily life. She is a proud pet momma to an elderly dog, a middle-aged cat, and a baby hedgehog. She wishes she had more time to write about her boring life, watch cat videos, dress up her hedgehog, and make gummy bear art.

FST! **Karyn Roberts-Hamilton** is a queer Tucson woman who loves cats, living in Tucson and smashing the patriarchy. She works in sexual health education and violence prevention at the University of Arizona and in the community. She and her partner April (mentioned in the story!) were married in March of 2017.

**Amy Robertson** got her bachelor's degree in Astronomy from the University of Arizona and she currently works as a Telescope Operator on Kitt Peak. Outside of work, she dances locally in Tucson with the Lajkonik Polish Dance Ensemble and The Barbea Williams Performing Company. She also directs her own personal dance project, Circuit, a contemporary dance company dedicated to exploring science through dance. In her free time, Amy reads ridiculously thick fantasy books and finds new ways to spoil her cat. She's a big fan of travel, loves to try new foods, and experience the variety the world has to offer.

**Theresa Sanders** is continual student of health, philosophy, nature, and mothering. She holds degrees in philosophy, nutrition, and public health. She has been a yoga teacher for over a decade and is passionate about the practice of mindfulness. She continues to try and understand how story and storytelling can help us make sense of health, illness, and community wellness.

As a sex educator, **Jessy Schmidt** spends a lot of time learning about all the fun, funky ways folks can enjoy each other's bodies and minds safely and consensually, so she can share this knowledge with the wider world through her classes and writing. Occasionally, she tells stories about the many mishaps she's had during the long, arduous learning process. She also walks her dogs a lot, eats doughnuts sometimes, and tries to read something Octavia Butler wrote at least once a year.

**Amanda Sierra** is a Tucson lifer who helps satiate the thirst of her fellow desert denizens with cocktails. She's probably suffering from a vitamin D deficiency due to working at night and writing during the day. She is definitely sleep deprived. Her son Jack is her favorite subject to write about. She never turns down a plate of spaghetti. She got married last December in an orange dress to the love of her life. The two have a beautiful Schnauzer mix named "Murray". Yes, after Bill.

(FST!) **Leigh D.C. Spencer** is the author of *Tequila and Cookies* – a poetry collection, and a co-author of *She Too – Four Voices in Almost Harmony*. Leigh is a storyteller who runs daily life through an irreverent filter to create honest, accessible pieces meant to make you laugh or cry out loud. She also has an impressive apron collection and enjoys making candy shaped like everything from brains to vaginas to mustaches. Leigh currently lives in Tucson, AZ with her hilarious and supportive husband, two inspirational sons, four rescue dogs, four turtles, a tankful of hermit crabs, and a big lizard named Levi. She joined the FST!erhood in December, 2015 and it felt like coming home. In a good way.

(FST!) **Penelope Starr** is a writer, founder and producer of Odyssey Storytelling, Executive Director of StoryArts Group, Inc., workshop presenter, community activist, citizen folklorist and restorer of Navajo rugs. She is the author of The Radical Act of Community Storytelling: Empowering Voices in Uncensored Events. See more about Penelope at http://www.penelopestarr.com

(FST!) **Anna Stokes** is a writer, in process of bursting into the world with a uniquely intersecting narrative of lifelong and authentic Jesus-following, casual sex, fatness, feminism, and social justice. She's also a hella awkward funny lady, a former radio show host and arts & culture journalist, a frequent storyteller, and a cat mom. In her free time, you can find her watching spooky YouTube vids, taking part in racial justice Bible studies, drinking funky cocktails, and applying to creative nonfiction MFAs.

(FST!)**Mrs. "Charli" Swinford** is a not-so-mild mannered insurance wonk by day, and a social justice activist, writer, storyteller, and humorist by night. In her free time she enjoys cooking, bicycling, gardening, and fitness. Her future goals are to change the world, destroy the gender binary, complete the book she has been writing for seven years, be named the U.S. ambassador to Antarctica, and finish painting the living room. Her short-term goals are to survive another year without enduring a mental competency hearing, and figure out where the beach that everyone enjoys long walks on is located.

(FST!) **Becca Tardiff** is a Tucson native, a fellow FST!er since 2012, and is still figuring out what she wants to be when she grows up. She enjoys soaking up the sunshine, playing hockey, eating nachos, and taking shameless #petselfies with her pups. If you see her around, she will ask to pet your dog.

As a PhD candidate, (FST!)**Thea** spends much time writing and much more time looking as if she were writing. She enjoys spending her spare time sailing in the San Francisco Bay, reading memoirs written in graphic novel format, hiking in Marin, making hummus, relaxing in prasarita padottanasana, studying mythology, and eating French food with her little sister.

(FST!) **Mo Urban** has performed all over Tucson and Phoenix and has hosted for Lauri Kilmartin at Laffs Comedy Club. She recently organized an all-female show at Tucson Improv Movement (TIM) where she hosted an amazing all-female lineup; she has also headlined at TIM and performed alongside storyteller Molly McCloy! Mo and Roxy Merrari run a comedy open mic at The Surly Wench Pub every 2nd Tuesday as well as a showcase every 4th Tuesday at 9 pm. Mo also recently started her own open mic at Café Passe every 3rd Wednesday of the month at 6pm. She loves comedy and loves the Tucson comedy scene. Mo is looking forward to growing and learning as a comedian and her biggest goal is to get better at comedy and support other women who want to do comedy.

(FST!)**Erin Whittig** spends her days in the University of Arizona Writing Program, and her nights in south Tucson, playing her cat's belly like a bongo. She rarely ventures outside of this idyllic bubble, but when she does, it's almost always for FST!

(FST!) **Lauren Wiggins** says: I was raised by women who could bend words to build structures and spaces, the likes of which you'd want to explore, some not for the faint of heart. All of my writing is dedicated to them, but I tell my stories for everyone who needs to hear they're not alone.

Made in the USA
Columbia, SC
10 June 2019